Lucia Jay von Seldene
Carolin Huder / Verena

111 places
in Berlin, that
you shouldn't miss

emons:

© Hermann-Josef Emons Verlag
All rights reserved
Editing: Carolin Huder
Texts: Lucia Jay von Seldeneck
Photographs: Verena Eidel
Maps: Regine Spohner
English translation: John Sykes
Printing and binding: B.O.S.S Druck and Medien GmbH, Goch
Printed in Germany 2013
ISBN 978-3-89705-853-8
First edition

For the latest information about emons, read our regular newsletter:
order it free of charge at
www.emons-verlag.de

Foreword

Berlin is crooked and jumbled, not smooth and shiny, and definitely not all of a piece. This becomes clear very quickly when you go in search of the places that define Berlin. Where do you start in a city that has no beginning and no end? What is typically Berlin about Berlin?

We started with our own favourite places – always the three of us, always with our city map, camera and notepad. We let ourselves drift into the furthest corners of this enormous, paradoxical city. And our zigzag paths kept taking us to new places: in which bar did David Bowie drink whisky, how do you find 11th Heaven in the concrete tower blocks of Marzahn, and where did the boatmen's pastor preach in the Westhafen?

On countless trips we gained a knack for discovering lively, unexpected places that are typical for Berlin. Every new square and every new street taught us that above all it is the people who give life to all these places – and their way of telling old and new stories. Berlin isn't a whole, it's a diversity. The 111 discoveries are home to images, stories and highly distinct moods. Here Berlin reveals itself to explorers.

In the end a single notepad wasn't enough: every new place triggers at least two more ideas. It takes hold of you. On fire! We can't get enough of these sparks – after all, they are supposed to be sparks of inspiration! There are no rules and guidelines for getting to know Berlin. You simply have to start. And stick at it. Because Berlin just keeps going on and on. So don't fall behind – go for it!

111 Orte

1 — 11th Heaven

The Princess's Boudoir in a tower block

The idea came from the children in the tower block. They wanted to show all the world that there is more to Marzahn than a bad reputation. And they succeeded: in 2004, with the support of the charity Kinderring Berlin, the children and youngsters set up Pension 11. Himmel (11th Heaven Guesthouse) right at the top of a concrete tower block with a plain façade of brown pebbles.

Since then they have been welcoming guests, cleaning the guest rooms and bathrooms, making breakfast – and showing visitors round their district.

You have to walk to 11th Heaven, as the lift only goes as far as the 10th floor. And the last steps take you to a Marzahn that surely astounds every visitor. Every room in the guesthouse is a world of its own – and tells a story from or about the district.

There is the Bed in the Cornfield, for example. Painted ears of golden-yellow corn sway all round the walls, poppies glow in between them, and there is a mill opposite the bed. And if you look out of the window across the residential high-rises, you really do see fields, hills and woods. Marzahn, the epitome of dreary concrete towers for many people, is right at the edge of the city, and is much greener and closer to nature than most districts in Berlin – something that few people know.

The other rooms in the guesthouse are called Bedded on Clouds and Princess's Boudoir. Not only places to sleep behind the doors in the corridor, however: the Fireplace Room was fitted out in honour of Prince Charles, who once visited Marzahn.

And in the Concrete Room the children have stripped all the walls bare so that you can read the date when the rough slabs were cast: 1984.

In the little dining room, the guest book lies open on the red-and-white checked tablecloth. One of the entries reads: »Marzahn has surprised us, in every way. We'll come again!«

Address Wittenberger Strasse 85, 12689 Berlin-Marzahn | Transport S 7 to Ahrensfelde; tram 16, 18 to Niemegker Strasse | Opening times Hochhauscafé Mon–Fri 10am–6pm, tel. 030/93772052, The Marzahn Matterhorn: this climbing wall made of recycled slabs from demolished buildings on Kemberger Strasse rises to a height of 17.5 metres (bring climbing gear with you!).

2 The Abandoned Iraqi Embassy

A bit of unfinished history

On the letterbox marked number 51, deep-brown rust is spreading from beneath the white paint. Below it a birch tree has squeezed through the posts of the fence and is now growing triumphantly on the other side.

All of which shows that a lot of time has gone by: what used to be the Iraqi embassy in East Berlin's former diplomatic quarter Pankow has been empty since 1991.

The doors of this shoe-box-shaped house with broad terraces at the front are wide open. Beyond them, the era when Saddam Hussein was the president of Iraq can still be seen, strewn over the floor on all storeys of the building: files full of documents, books, papers, coffee filters and letter paper. On a burnt table there stands a typewriter with Arabic letters on the keys, and two mouldy armchairs are still arranged around a coffee table in a room with a view of the overgrown garden.

It is well known that the GDR maintained a close relationship to Iraq – links that seemed to have economic advantages for both sides. Iraq possessed oil, and the GDR had armaments.

During the Gulf War in 1991, all Iraqi diplomats were ordered to leave Germany. Since then the building has been deserted. The question of ownership remains to be settled. The land belongs to the Federal Republic of Germany. Iraq still has the right to use the site, but appears to have no real interest in doing so. The new Iraqi embassy is situated in Zehlendorf – on the other side of the city.

The three storeys of this 1970s concrete structure in Pankow have become a cult space for photographers, film makers and other inquisitive persons. Time has stood still – while grass and moss cover the chairs, stairs and piles of documents. That is one way of coming to terms with the past.

Address Tschaikowskistrasse 51, 13156 Berlin-Pankow | Transport Tram M 1, bus 107, 250, both to Tschaikowskistrasse; bus 150, 155 to Homayerstrasse | Tip Schloss Schöneweide: further along Tschaikowskistrasse is the VIP guesthouse of the GDR. Fidel Castro, Indira Gandhi and Mikhail Gorbachev are among those who stayed here.

3 Alt-Lübars

A place to slow down

Petrol stations, DIY stores and fast-food outlets whizz past at high speed on the main road out of the city. But all at once, you hit the brakes: bumpy cobblestones, elongated single-storey houses, the smell of horses. It takes you by surprise: in Alt-Lübars you are suddenly in the middle of an old village green, surrounded by fields and meadows.

This city has many village centres. It took a long time for Berlin to become a great metropolis – and it did so by means of a trick. When Greater Berlin was established, it incorporated 59 rural communes, 27 manors and seven towns at a stroke in 1920. By this means it increased in size 14 times from one day to the next, and became the world's third-largest city after New York and London – but still consisted of villages and countryside for the most part. And today these old village centres remain the focus of activity. The village streets have become the main shopping streets of city districts, and you can buy everything locally – there is no need to travel »to Berlin«, as people put it.

Alt-Lübars is the only one of these places whose appearance has not changed. Thanks to a campaign by the villagers there is no supermarket on the church square and no drugstore next to the village pub Alter Dorfkrug. To this day, life here takes its character from agriculture.

In the days when it was part of West Berlin, Alt-Lübars was regarded as almost exotic – in a city surrounded by a wall, Berliners came here in order to see farmers at work. When the village then gained protected status and its surroundings became a nature reserve, that was the end of the farms.

But in Alt-Lübars a way was found of saving the village and its idyllic character: the old farmyards were converted to stables for horse-riding. Today 150 people live around the old church – and some 300 mares, stallions and geldings.

Address Alt-Lübars, 13469 Berlin-Reinickendorf | Transport Bus 222 to Alt-Lübars | Tip Kräuterhof Lübars: herbs, fruit and vegetables straight from the fields round about are sold on the village green.

4 Animal Town

Eyeball to eyeball

Exposed concrete, shallow pools of water, and above all lots of open space. If this place were right next to the Chancellery in the government quarter it would not catch the eye. But here at the edge of the city, where pasture and arable land begin, and the last areas of housing are crowded together, this futuristic complex is highly conspicuous.

»Stadt der Tiere« (Animal Town) in Falkenberg, an area equivalent to 30 football pitches, is a temporary home for about 1200 abandoned animals. The architecture is entirely adapted to the residents – which makes it possible for humans and animals to encounter each other in a new and direct way.

The rabbit hutches are at eye level, so you don't have to bend down to look for pet in its cage on the floor. This does indeed create a new way of getting close to the animals, because visitors shrink, as it were, into the dimensions of the rabbit world.

The cat home is another example: when you walk along the corridor, cats are sitting in their rooms to left and right on armchairs, in baskets or even on a doll's bed. Cheerful music comes from a cassette recorder. This is more than just accommodation for animals – they live well here.

As in a zoo, arrow-shaped signs in the courtyard point the way to the bird house, the dogs, the exotic animals. The openness of the buildings as they were first planned turned out not to be possible. The architecture gave the animals too little opportunity to seek refuge. And the frightened creatures who are brought here often need plenty of care and rest at first. Now, however, there are separate, quiet areas for the new arrivals and the longer-term residents.

From the canine quarters, dog walkers come across the yard. Sometimes these unpaid volunteers have their work cut out to manage the dogs' unrestrained joy at being taken for a walk. But both the dogs and the animals seem to enjoy it.

Address Hausvaterweg 39, 13057 Berlin-Hohenschönhausen | Transport Bus 197 to Tier-heim Berlin | Opening times Mon–Fri 11am–5pm, Sat, Sun 11am–4pm | Tip North of Falkenberg at the north-eastern edge of the city, liquid sewage from Berlin was deposited on symmetrical plots of land in the 19th century. Today it is a large nature reserve.

5__Antique Building Material

Liebchen's sanctuary for Berlin's treasures

Those colourful mosaic stones, for example. They have been sorted by colour, and on each pile a yellowing photo is propped showing the picture that these countless angular stones once formed: a saint's image on the wall of a villa in Dahlem. When the house was torn down, the colourful stones were almost lost in the rubble, and the photo of how they were arranged was nearly forgotten.

Almost everything in this yard shares the fate of having been rescued at the eleventh hour. Removed from their context, the doors and door handles, balcony railings and tiled ovens, stair balustrades and gas lamps tell a fragmentary tale of old Berlin. Wolfram Liebchen knows every story. He has jotted down the place of origin and the age of the things on white paper notes. The prices in the yard are not only calculated according to the material and its condition, but also according to its historical value.

Liebchen calls himself a treasure hunter. When the authorities demolished whole quarters of old buildings in the 1960s, protests against this »scorched-earth redevelopment« became more and more vociferous. In the 1980s the old houses were no longer destroyed, but thoroughly cleared out. The tiled stoves were knocked out of their corners, parquet floors and floor boards, tiles and even plaster decorations were thrown into the rubbish skip – if Wolfram Liebchen didn't come and take them away.

His best excavation site was the Adlon. After the war the GDR levelled the ruins of this famous hotel and border guards patrolled the site. When the Wall fell and the new Adlon was planned, Liebchen went along with the demolition contractors – and found marble treasures in the rubble.

Today architects and construction workers phone him when antique material is to be thrown away. His treasures come to rest in the yard behind a high stone wall – and sooner or later they find a new home, usually in Berlin.

Address Lehrter Strasse 25/26, 10557 Berlin-Tiergarten | **Transport** Bus 123 to Krupp-strasse | **Opening times** Wed, Sat 10am–2pm and by appointment, tel. 030/3943093 | **Tip** History park: Follow Lehrter Strasse towards Hauptbahnhof to reach the accessible prison memorial site called Zellengefängnis Lehrter Strasse.

6___The Apartment of Kommune 1
Where the revolution was practised

One day it finally ran out of steam. The attempt to find an alternative to the bourgeois nuclear family had no energy left. Between 1967 and 1969 Kommune 1 moved from one place to another in Berlin four times – until it settled for its last year in brick-built premises in a back yard in Moabit. The experiment of establishing a new form of living together with equal rights, which had such a fundamental influence on society, simply came to an end after a year here in Stephanstrasse.

It was one floor of an old felt factory, and seemed to be the right place for the scheme to start a political revolution in the private sphere. In the communal life of the large room with tall windows, no petit bourgeois separation existed. The group was the focus, freedom was the doctrine. Lots of visitors came, lots of journalists – and even Jimi Hendrix dropped in.

Soon, however, everything revolved around Uschi Obermeier and Rainer Langhans. The newspapers came and took photos of the commune. And the two stars of the commune scene talked about their relationship and their sexuality. Deep cracks appeared in the big dream of a new form of society: drug addiction and quarrels reduced the size of the group – and finally in 1969 the apartment was raided and trashed by a gang of rockers.

The large windows subdivided into small squares, which can be seen on photos from the days of the commune, are still there, but no longer in the apartment that was occupied by Kommune 1. The original windows are used as partitions in the flat at the top of the building.

It and the first floor are now apartments for tourists. Visitors to Berlin like to stay here, not only because it is so quiet in this green back yard in the middle of the city, but also because of the history of Kommune 1, which had an impact on many visitors in the 1960s – and fundamentally changed them.

Address Stephanstrasse 60, 10559 Berlin-Tiergarten | Transport Bus M 27, 123 to Stenda-
ler Strasse | Opening times Private premises; please make contact via www.berlinlofts.com |
Tip The Arminius-Markthalle: beneath old vaults at Arminiusstrasse 2–4 good wine, crafts
and local products are on sale.

7 _ The AVUS Motel
Where records are kept

Like a stormy sea, traffic rages around the disused north curve of the »Automobil-Verkehrs- und Übungs-Strasse« (automobile, traffic and practice road), better known as AVUS. This island in the middle of the urban highway can only be reached via its own exit or through a tunnel from the nearest subway station. When you have found the way through, you can take a leisurely walk along the broad, gently sloping curve of asphalt on which records were once set. Inside the curve, where trucks park in dense rows today, up to 50,000 spectators at motor races were once captivated by the thrill of speed.

At the edge of the north curve stands what used to be the Mercedes viewing tower and is now the AVUS Motel. The view from the four galleries around it has remained the same: cars roar past and dwindle at the end of the arrow-straight road to little specks in the distance.

On the other side of the autobahn is the grandstand, today with deserted rows of bench seats and abandoned flagpoles, however.

The motel is a place of melancholy memories of the time when fans of motor racing from all over the world gathered here at the north curve. Races were held on the straight as late as the 1990s. Today truckers and workers from the trade-fair site come to the diner.

When the windows are tilted open, you can hear the cars zoom by. This is not a bleak place, however: it tells of great achievements and triumphs. On the tables under sheets of glass, newspaper cuttings and photos have been lovingly arranged to form collages.

Table for table you can read the highlights of the history of the AVUS. For many Berliners one of the greatest moments was the opening of the 10-kilometre race track for everybody in 1921. People paid a handsome sum of money for a drive along the smooth surface: ten marks for a one-way trip – or a three-month season ticket for 1000 marks.

Address A 115, Messedamm exit, 14057 Berlin-Charlottenburg | Transport S 9, S 75 to Westkreuz; bus 219 to Messegelände | Tip The hidden AVUS memorial: behind the car park, a little further along the autobahn, you reach a memorial stone on the race track.

8 The Ballroom in Grünau

Berlin's abandoned Riviera

In the 1920s the people of Berlin flocked to the banks of the river Dahme. They garbed themselves in fashionable dresses and elegant suits, and boarded gaily lit steamboats to sail out to their riviera, in Grünau.

Filled with expectancy for the evening ahead, they disembarked at the pier and entered palm-fringed gardens. It was a period when Berlin devoted itself to entertainment as never before. More than 200 dance halls and pleasure palaces vied with each other in their splendour, magnificence and glamour. And this way of life is tangible here: the beauty and opulence have remained – despite decay, weathering and vandalism. Visitors are almost reverent at the sight of this ensemble by the water, sunk in silence and completely undisturbed.

The most impressive feature of the Riviera ballroom is its dimensions. To describe this riverside place of entertainment simply as a »place for a trip out« might be misleading. Glittering balls were once held in this room on the shining dance floor beneath weighty chandeliers. A veranda runs all the way around it. Those who stood here could either cast their eyes over the dancers or gaze across the water outside. It is not difficult to imagine all of this: a little decaying pomp in the deserted rooms, a bit of crumbling plasterwork on the staircase, and the delightful slopes of the riverbank – that is all it takes for your imagination to supply the missing details in what you see.

In the GDR period this place lost its splendour but not its importance. Thousands of trippers went out to Grünau at weekends. A fallen tree in the garden has been lying there for many years. Little birches, the trees that grow fastest here, have sprung up around it. Right at the back in the charming garden there is a small pavilion. The music has fallen silent, but a romantic aura still envelops this spot on the riverbank.

Address Regattastrasse, between Büxensteinallee and Libboldallee, 12527 Berlin-Köpenick | **Transport** S 8, S 85 to Grünau; tram 68; bus 163, 263, 363 to Grünau station | **Tip** Tram route 68: what used to be the Schmöckwitz-Grünauer Uferbahn is now probably Berlin's most attractive tram route, from Alt-Köpenick to Alt-Schmöckwitz.

9__The Barbrücke at Night

A test of courage beneath the stars

At night the bridge is completely dark – the row of lamps along Barstrasse simply comes to an end at the bridge. This means that, when you lean on the balustrade here, you can do something that is otherwise impossible in the middle of the city: you can immerse yourself in the night.

The balustrade of the Barbrücke is built of solid stone, as if it had been built to ward off something that lurks behind. When you peer over you are confronted with a comprehensive, threatening darkness, but above there is suddenly a clear view of the stars, and below you water shines from the black depths.

You can feel the night with all your senses: an instinctive awareness carries you along. Somewhere behind the trees an animal rustles and a frog croaks. Beneath the bridge flows the elongated watercourse called Fennsee, the tip of an ice-age channel that has been made into a park. The ice age – unimaginably distant, a thought as dark and menacing as the view down into this primeval river valley today.

After leaning for a while on the bridge balustrade, your inner excitement calms down – and you begin to enjoy the unaccustomed tranquillity. The nightingales encourage you in this – for it is nightingales with their strange melodies that rule the darkness on the Barbrücke from May until mid-June. Down here there are no sounds to disturb their calls of courtship.

If the view down from the bridge is not enough, you can immerse yourself completely in the world of darkness below it. To undertake this test of courage you have to find the little path at its north-western end.

Steps lead down, into the heart of the night. From a projection at the bridge wall, a narrow walkway leads to the further bank of the Fennsee. From here you go up to the road, to the city lights – where the adventure ends!

Address Barstrasse, 10713 Berlin-Wilmersdorf | **Transport** S 41, S 42, S 46, U 3 to Heidelberger Platz; bus 101, 249 to Am Volkspark | **Tip** A night walk: carry on walking through the Volkspark. Beyond the big duck pond at the end of the park is the illuminated subway station Rathaus Schöneberg – one of the most beautiful in the city.

10_ The Bat Cellar
A world upside down

They keep themselves to themselves, but little Natterer's bats are loyal creatures. For five years they have been coming to their regular spot to hibernate undisturbed and alone – in the castle toilet of the Royal Bastion of the citadel in Spandau. Each November they hook themselves onto the icy stone in a windowless chamber with a single claw – and stay suspended above the royal latrine until the weather gets warmer.

Word has spread that the cracks and crevices of the old stone wall in the citadel are an ideal place to hook onto and hang out. As many as 10,000 bats spend the winter in the vaults of the castle. This number is only an estimate, as it is not possible to look inside all the cracks, openings and hollow places. In summer, on the other hand, the castle is deserted and empty, as the hibernating bats fly away in swarms and do not return to their favourite dwelling place in the moated castle until autumn.

In the bat cellar on the other side of the castle courtyard, however, you can watch small nocturnal flying mammals all year round. In a low passage beneath wide heating pipes, a nature protection society called Artenschutz Team has set up a bat exhibition. The main attraction can be seen behind large sheets of glass. It starts off as a fluttering.

It is dark inside the bat compound, but after a while you can make out Egyptian fruit bats and smaller Seba's short-tailed bats, hanging from thick ropes and flying from niche to niche. One cellar door further along there is a true rarity: Cuban nectar bats, small white animals that live only from the nectar of flowering plants. In Cuba they live in great swarms – and the only other place where they can be seen is here in Spandau.

In the evening the fluttering behind glass comes to an end. Lights are switched on in the cellar rooms – and the bats go to sleep.

Address Am Juliusturm 64, 13599 Berlin-Spandau | Transport S 9, S 75 to Spandau; U 7, bus X 33 to Zitadelle Spandau | Opening times Mon–Sun 10am–5pm for the exhibition and tropical bats; for guided tours in the vaults of the citadel, tel. 030/36750061 or www.bat-ev.de | Tip Bat boxes: as bat habitats are becoming scarcer, Artenschutz Team in Berlin have produced instructions for building bat boxes.

11 — The Berberis by the Panke

Healing power in the past and present

Wedding doesn't have a reputation for being idyllic. It is the part of Berlin where the proletariat made history – but in this workers' quarter there is a shortage of work. The street scene in Wedding is characterized by large Turkish families, corner pubs that open 24 hours a day and beauty studios.

But there is one idyllic spot in the otherwise rough north-west of the city: the river Panke. On its banks, where healing springs attracted Berliners to the Luisenbad spa outside the city gates in the 18th century, an unjustly forgotten healing plant grows: the berberis, also known as barberry.

At Travemünder Strasse the Panke flows beneath Badstrasse. At first you really have to search for it, as in a city with five-storey apartment buildings, four-lane roads and double-decker buses, this little watercourse with its curving bridges is hardly entitled to be called a river.

If you take the path on its banks from Badstrasse going north, you will be surprised by hidden splendour on the right: KAFÈ KÜCHE, proclaim the letters on the façade of what was once a place of entertainment. Today this is a municipal library, and inside it is worth looking at the pictures of the former Luisenbad spa.

As you continue along the stream, the city and its noise recede into the distance – and other things become important. About 100 metres beyond Osloer Strasse you will make a discovery on the left bank of the Panke: a berberis bush about three metres in diameter.

In times of need, the sour red berries on this shrub, which is usually trimmed to form a hedge, were often used as a substitute for lemons. Berberis adds a touch of tartness to jam. The berries and the bark of the roots are said to be high in vitamin C, and also to have healing properties. But beware: the flowers and leaves are poisonous! The berries can be harvested from late September.

Address Travemünderstrasse / Badstrasse, 13357 Berlin-Wedding | **Transport** U 8 to Pank-strasse or Osloer Strasse; bus 125, 128, 150, 255 to Osloer Strasse subway station | **Tip** Foraging: if you like the taste of barberries, go to www.mundraub.org to find more wild fruit trees in Berlin.

12__ The Berlin Room
Occupying a free space

It lies at the far end of the corridor, and is a peculiarity of Berlin – a kind of transitional zone, an undefined intermediate space, a free area in the middle of a rational, late 19th-century house.

In this period apartments in Berlin were often enlarged by breaking through the wall into the side wing. The »Berlin room« is the extension of the corridor from which the kitchen and the maid's room could be reached.

It connected the finer rooms in the apartment with the workaday part at the back, the part where the family normally did not go. This made it difficult to find a purpose for this long-drawn-out passage, which to make things worse was dark, as the only window was in the far corner and looked out to the backyard.

It must have been like this for the Heyn family, too. The rattan manufacturer Fritz Heyn built this house in 1893 and moved into the genteel piano nobile with his wife and their 16 children. Today visitors to the rooms in the Museumswohnung (museum apartment) in Pankow gaze around in amazement: Baroque gilded plasterwork, superb ceiling paintings, tiled stoves with gold decoration, chandeliers – all slumbering behind drawn curtains for protection. And at the end of this, when you turn the corner, the significance of the Berlin room for the inhabitants becomes apparent.

In the Heyn home, as in so many apartments in Berlin, this space gradually became the centre of the household. The family did not dine in the salon or sit together in the drawing room every day. These places were reserved for special occasions. The Berlin room with its artistically painted linoleum floor became the dining and living room.

And even more than that: this once-neglected middle part of the corridor superseded the rooms that were designed to impress. The atmosphere was simply cosier here, the light less bright – and people felt freer.

Address Museumswohnung Pankow, Heynstrasse 8, 13187 Berlin-Pankow | **Transport** S 1, S 25, S 85 to Wollankstrasse; S 2, S 8, S 9, U 2 to Pankow; bus M 27, 250 to Görschstrasse | **Opening times** Tue, Thu, Sun 10am–6pm, tel. 030/4814047 | **Tip** The former goods railway station of Pankow-Heinersdorf: the old turntable building, the big locomotive shed and the office building at Pankow station are open for flora, fauna and explorers.

13__Berlin's Balcony
This is summer

Threaded like beads at regular intervals, cars leave the city. Berlin ends here. The sheds of DIY stores and new residential estates line the arterial road. And between all of this, as if framed by eyesores at the margins of the city, is a view of fields, woods and lakes stretching as far as the Müggelberg hills in the far south.

Thanks to this view, Berlin's balcony deserves its name: on the Barnim Plateau blue cornflowers and red poppies add dots of colour to the edge of fields, and beyond it lies the lush green of Berlin's primeval river valley.

The balcony at home is sacred for Berliners. It is a patch of freedom, to which everyone has a right. There are no rules about using it or shaping it. So the principle is: all or nothing!

Everyone subscribes to a common philosophy, which is linked to a new word that has been coined: Balconia. Balconia describes the feeling of stepping outside, taking a deep breath, and putting your feet up on the railing.

In this respect too the massive »balcony« at the edge of the city lives up to its name. It radiates calm. After all, it was formed millions of years ago.

And since then it has been what balconies for the most part really are: a transition between inside and outside, between the private and the public or, as here, between the city and the country.

And the view across this gentle slope, the steepest gradient in Berlin, makes everyone aware of one thing: what would summer in Berlin be without all of this? The green spaces, the endless sky and above all the abundance of large and small lakes.

Nestling deeply in forests or meadows, for Berliners they are the true natural source. No mountain hike and no beach holiday gives stressed city-dwellers more profound relaxation than swimming in the middle of a quiet, lonely lake. You feel summer in its entirety – and become part of it.

Address Alt-Mahlsdorf, at the hotel »An der Weide« – 12623 Berlin-Hellersdorf | Transport S5 to Mahlsdorf (10 minutes' walk) | Tip Panoramic walk: the trail along the Barnim-hang passes through three historic villages: Alt-Biesdorf, Alt-Kaulsdorf and Mahlsdorf.

14_ The Bieberbau

Hospitality in a master craftsman's house

His identity is unknown. Pleased with himself and the world, he grins at you, wearing an expression of happy intoxication. Above him two monkeys are climbing about on a wooden beam. They are peering at the tables as if at any moment they will jump down and start taking the food from the plates.

However, they stay where they are with a greedy look, because they are made of plaster. Like so many other figures in the room – the cow that peeps out from between the wooden supports and the Greek gods that populate the wall between cypresses and columns. Not even the black-painted half-timbering on the walls is genuine. There is a reason why every wall in this restaurant in Wilmersdorf is adorned up to the ceiling.

This was once the workshop and showroom of the court stucco craftsman Richard Bieber. In the late 19th century he and his employees created this impressive sculptural world inside the house and on its façade. Bieber portrayed himself twice in these scenes from fables.

Later, too, this house was a home for artists. In the 20th century Max Pechstein and Ernst-Ludwig Kirchner, among others, moved in – and the wonderfully decorated rooms at the front of the house became the Bieberbau, a pub where Berlin's artistic crowd liked to meet.

The splendour of its bourgeois affluence survived the years, outliving not only the period of »deplastering« in the 1920s, when every fancy flourish met with disapproval. Miraculously the tendrils and figures in the Bieberbau also survived the blast of a bomb during the war that completely destroyed the façade of the house.

When you have had enough of ancient times, mythology and the gods of wine, you can turn your attention to the food. The meals served in the Bieberbau are exquisite – and full of surprises: three courses here sometimes turn into six, seven or eight.

Address Durlacher Strasse 15, 10715 Berlin-Wilmersdorf | Transport S 41, S 42, S 46, U 9 to Bundesplatz; bus 248 to Wexstrasse | Opening times Tue–Sat 6pm–midnight, booking tel. 030/8532390, www.bieberbau-berlin.de | Tip The Rias broadcasting house: today this protected monument by the Volkspark is home to Deutschlandradio. Just follow the road as far as Hans-Rosenthal-Platz.

15__ The Bierpinsel
A sign of the times

Angular, bulky and, it has to be admitted, somehow misshapen, it towers above the traffic intersection over a two-lane shopping street in Steglitz. Here the street Schlossstrasse, above which the autobahn approach was placed like a colossus, lies in an eternally dark shadow. But above it rises the Bierpinsel, like a gigantic cabin on a stick, or perhaps a paintbrush, which is what »Pinsel« means.

When this red tower was opened in 1976, lots of free beer flowed – and from that moment the new landmark in Steglitz had acquired its name.

The »tower-art« project named Turmkunst 2010 undertook to liven up this tower, which had been proclaimed dead, and temporarily its three storeys glowed in many colours. And the colours and street-art motifs on the outside of the tower have at least made Berliners aware of the Bierpinsel again. Its modern Pop architecture ceased to be chic long ago, and for years it seemed to have been forgotten. It was left over. For years it has not been possible to find anyone to run the restaurant.

This is the fate of most buildings from this period. They are nobody's darlings. There is not even a name for this style of Berlin postwar architecture. At present a term that is used by both its fans and opponents seems to be gaining acceptance: »Berliner Restmoderne«, left-over Modernism.

The architects of the Bierpinsel, Ralf Schüler and Ursulina Schüler-Witte, designed a number of other city landmarks in the same style, for example the Internationales Congress Centrum, ICC for short.

Although many people condemn this style as »concrete Modernism« and »Brutalism«, and would like to see it erased from the cityscape, these buildings will undoubtedly still have admirers when parts of the new Potsdamer Platz and the numerous shoe-box-style shopping centres on Alexanderplatz have long been forgotten.

Address Schlossstrasse 17, 12163 Berlin-Steglitz | Transport U 9 to Schlossstrasse; bus M 48, M 85, 186, 282 to Schlossstrasse subway station | Tip Schlossstrasse subway station: designed by the architects of the Bierpinsel, this station is a true trip back in time to the 1970s thanks to its shapes, colours and structures.

16 __ The Black-and-White Photo Machine

It's over in a flash

They look like completely normal booths for taking passport photos – and completely normal photo booths is what they are, except that for unfathomable reasons they have become cult sites in Berlin. »Take your own photo!«, proclaims the sign next to the dark, wavy mirror. And a further sign in the booth says: »Please consider the neighbours by staying quiet after 11 pm!« Taking photos of yourself is seemingly a noisy business.

This is because word has spread. For only two euros you can capture your memories on a black-and-white strip of photos. Which is why people come to the booth – couples, exchange students, colleagues, party-goers, parents, children and people on their way home. They wait alone or in groups in front of the machine until it has ejected the previous customers' photos and it is their turn at last.

Inside the booth chaos reigns at first until everyone has found a place around the revolving seat. Heads try to squeeze a bit further into the middle of the picture, and then everyone concentrates on the flash. After the first shot, the mood is a little more relaxed. The second flash comes unexpectedly quickly, and the third seems to take a long time. Most people have an incredulous expression for the last shot. Then out they get and wait. The calm before the storm: when the strip of photos appears, there is no holding back the pent-up excitement.

One popular practice is to write messages on sheets of paper, one word after the other, and to hold up one sheet for every photo so that the whole sentence can be read at the end on the strip of prints. But the real reason why black-and-white prints are so well loved is very simple: you always look good on them. The slightly over-exposed photos show a regular and clear face, with no rings round the eyes and no wrinkles. A beautiful memory in every way.

Address Kastanienallee 98, 10435 Berlin-Prenzlauer Berg | **Transport** U 2 to Eberswalder Strasse; tram M 1, 12 to Eberswalder Strasse subway station | **Tip** Photocopier: the nearest copy shop is at the corner of Kastanienallee and Oderberger Strasse – to avoid any arguments about the best photo!

17__The Bücherwald
Recommended reading

They don't catch the eye. They stand by the side of the road as if they have always been there and as if they will be there for ever: five thick, old tree trunks. But there is something strange about them. In the space of a mere five minutes a man with a dog, two Italians with rucksacks and an elderly couple have walked directly up to them and examined them attentively from all sides. As they do so, they all move their heads, tilted at a slight angle, downwards along the trunks. Inside the trees, behind transparent plastic flaps, there is indeed something to see: books.

The books are in small, hollowed-out compartments, and the people who stop here take them out, leaf through them – and sometimes spontaneously stuff a book into a shopping bag and take it away with them.

This is how the circulation of books works in the Bücherwald (»book forest«): someone removes a volume – and someone else brings along another and puts it in the space that has become free. This book exchange is part of a worldwide movement that describes itself as »bookcrossing«. The motto is: give a new life to your books instead of leaving them on the shelf.

After all, there is reading matter to suit every situation in life. Three titles chosen at random from the book forest in Prenzlauer Berg are »Space, Earth, Humanity«, »Economics for Educators« and »The Lord's Mistress«.

And if you take this idea of passing on books seriously, you can give your book an ID number, which then appears on the bookcrossers' homepage. After that you can leave your book lying around anywhere – on a bench, in the subway, at a beach or swimming pool. Whoever finds it – if he or she is initiated into the system – registers the book's next stopping-place on the internet site, and in this way its wanderings can be followed. Yes, it really works! See www.bookcrossing.de.

Address Sredzkistrasse / Kollwitzstrasse, 10435 Berlin-Prenzlauer Berg | **Transport** U2 to Eberswalder Strasse; tram M10 to Husemannstrasse; tram M2 to Marienburger Strasse; bus 115 to Sredzkistrasse | **Tip** Café Anna Blume: a genuine tip for insiders thanks to its home-baked cakes – and you can watch the book-swappers from the table by the window.

18 Burg am See

The Turkish beer garden by the canal

A German corner pub next to a Turkish tea-shop, a Turkish green-grocer next to a German supermarket – this is a perfectly normal scene on the streets of Kreuzberg and Neukölln. Nevertheless, usually it is a case of one alongside the other: a blend of German and Turkish culture is rarely to be seen.

However, on the Landwehrkanal, where waters from Kreuzberg, Neukölln and Treptow meet, this mixing does exist. White sun-shades advertising German Paulaner beer provide shade.

Families, both German and Turkish, sit at the beer-garden tables. Children run up and down the hedges. In the middle of the garden, teenagers sit and share a shisha. Over their heads its fruity smoke mingles with the spicy smell of hearty food that wafts over from the barbecue. The aroma of fresh pizza, and a somewhat greasier contribution from the fat in which the French fries are cooked, add to the mixture. At the counter there is German wheat beer – or tea from a big samovar.

All over the world, beer gardens are known as a truly German phenomenon. And equally, tea gardens are as Turkish as it gets. Here on the canal bank these two traditions with their typical habits and customs blend in one single place: a family tea-and-beer garden with a view of the water. One couple are sitting opposite each other – she eating French fries, he cracking sunflower seeds. The warm summer evening passes with pleasant slowness.

A fountain splashes in the middle of the garden. Guests are assured that this is a wishing-well for lovers. Though with no guarantee. What is guaranteed here, however, is that two cultures come closer, and that people sit next to each other on the benches in a way that rarely happens so naturally and by chance in Kreuzberg. Perhaps this has something to do with the big wooden castle in which German and Turkish children climb around together – until their parents return to the tables with their trays.

Address Ratiborstrasse 14c, 10999 Berlin-Kreuzberg | Transport Bus M29, 171, 194 to Pflügerstrasse | Opening times In the beer-garden season daily 10am–10pm | Tip Table tennis: on the canal bank you can challenge experts to a game.

19__ The Cafeteria in the Bürgeramt

Fresh meatballs and an all-round view

The free view all the way to the horizon refreshes the eyes and the soul. A view across fields, a lake or the sea is said to have a calming effect. In the city, such an unimpeded view is only to be had over the rooftops. From the cafeteria in the Bürgeramt (city offices) in Kreuzberg, for example. As in every canteen, the furnishings are above all utilitarian. Plain, eggshell-coloured tables for four with dark brown wooden chairs, a shelf for indoor plants as a partition, and the trolleys on which to place returned trays next to the counter where the food is served.

The special thing about this cafeteria is outside: the sky. In every direction. Your eyes linger for a moment on a church tower or Potsdamer Platz – but then they can roam. Beneath you are red-brown roofs, and below them canyon-like streets with tiny cars creeping along and the bustle of tiny people at the crossroads.

The food here is down-to-earth. The favourites are home-made meatballs, stews and of course a mug of coffee. Up here, it will be a long time before latte macchiato to go replaces the good old mug of coffee. And at the neighbouring tables a local speciality is thrown in: all around people shout and rant in the immaculate Berlin dialect that is used for arguments in pubs. At breakfast time it is mainly elderly people from the neighbourhood, making comments about the newspaper that they have spread out on the table in front of them, and reading aloud the best bits, including the special offers from supermarket advertisements. Later the employees of the city offices come here to eat their lunch – and, whether you want to or not, you find out what happened that morning behind the doors on the long corridors. In this way you certainly keep your feet firmly on the ground here – even if the view of the skies all around might give a different impression.

Address Bezirksamt Friedrichshain-Kreuzberg, Yorckstrasse 4–11, 10965 Berlin-Kreuzberg | **Transport** U 6, U 7 to Mehringdamm; bus M 19, 140 to Yorckstrasse / Grossbeerenstrasse | **Opening times** Mon–Fri breakfast 7–11am, lunch 11am–3pm | **Tip** The Kreuzberg: walk along Mehringdamm to Kreuzbergstrasse, then climb to the summit of the Kreuzberg, one of the tallest hills in the city, in Viktoriapark.

20__The Capitol

The cinema in a living room

Keeping a genteel distance, entirely untouched by the events of the world, the fine houses of Dahlem sleep undisturbed in the shade of mature trees, surrounded by rhododendrons. The house next to the main building of the Freie Universität Berlin, for example. It looks like many of the houses in this neighbourhood: box-like, with a vine growing up its light-coloured two-storey façade. If it were not for the signage above the terrace, no-one would ever guess that inside, in the impressive piano nobile of this residence, there is a cinema.

Its history, too, is known to few: Prof. Carl Fröhlich, president of the Reichsfilmkammer, which controlled the cinema industry in the Nazi period, had a room for private viewings built here in 1942 in his villa in Dahlem.

For three years this inconspicuous house on Thielallee was the final court of judgment at which the Nazis viewed new and old films, and decided what German audiences were permitted to see – and what was not allowed. There was no escaping this controlling body. Everyone who wanted to take part in any way in film productions in the Third Reich had to become a member of the Reichsfilmkammer. The Nazis really succeeded in doing what had been thought impossible: gaining control of art.

Today old film posters hang up to the ceiling above the curved staircase in the Capitol. And, if as they were witnesses to a tacit reconciliation, the titles of films that were banned during the Third Reich catch the eye: Charlie Chaplin's »Goldrush«, for example, and »Les Enfants du Paradis«.

The Capitol has a reputation as an especially charming arthouse cinema, with select films – and style: the coffee is not served in paper cups here, and many people come a little earlier to enjoy a glass of wine in the evening sun. It almost seems as if the guests had been invited personally, first for a drink on the terrace – and later to watch a film in the living room.

Address Thielallee 36, 14195 Berlin-Zehlendorf | **Transport** U 3 to Thielplatz; bus 110 to Löhleinstrasse | **Opening times** Tel. 030/8316417 for the latest programme | **Tip** The dome of the Reichstag is not the only one by Norman Foster: he designed a dome for a library, the Philologische Bibliothek, right next to the cinema at Habelschwerdter Allee 45.

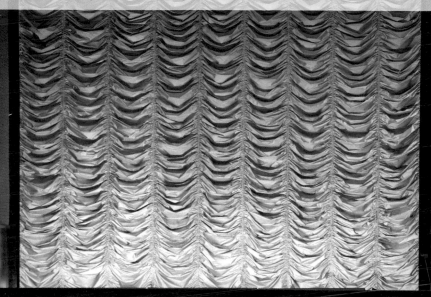

21__City of Science
Staying top

The longer you look up at these two big heads, which move almost imperceptibly but never cease to rotate about their own axis, the clearer it becomes why they stand here in Berlin-Adlershof. The panels that make up the faces are shifting, and the smooth, regular features become unrecognisable from one moment to the next, then they rotate, and finally they appear completely abstract – only to turn back to the accustomed shape again after a while.

The two faces captivate you with their tension, their constant changes – and there is a good reason why they have become a symbol for the Stadt der Wissenschaft, the city of science, economics and media in Adlershof.

You can feel the pioneering spirit here as if it were tangible. If you walk around a little in the City of Science, you will recognise a highly symbolic image in this organically grown ensemble of modern and historic buildings: as in a great laboratory, where people are investigating, developing, rejecting and starting all over again the whole time, the buildings have grown around each other, support each other and nevertheless allow each other the freedom that they need.

The gigantic wind tunnel and the aerodynamic tower are particularly impressive. Even today. When they were built in the 1930s, these two historic plants in the centre for flight technology in Johannisthal-Adlershof were at the forefront globally.

The City of Science has always been about staying at the top – with the RoboCup, for example. At these annual world championships of artificial intelligence, the aim is much more than just to score goals.

Scientists from all over the world meet here to present the autonomous actions of and communication between their robots by getting them to play football against each other. After all, football is accepted globally as an undisputed form of natural selection.

Address Rudower Chaussee, near number 24, 12489 Berlin-Treptow | **Transport** S 8, 9, 45, 46, 85 to Adlershof; bus 163, 164 to Walther-Nernst-Strasse | **Tip** A tour of the site – without a guide, opening times or hurry – enables everyone to explore the Stadt der Wissenschaften for themselves. The first stage starts at Adlershof railway station.

22 ___ The Climbing Tree
Capri for the soul

If you leave the ground here, you won't regret it. Up there nobody will disturb you. Nobody will see you, while you enjoy wonderful views in all directions through the peep-holes.

The climbing tree in the Bürgerpark, the »citizens' park«, is not hard to find if you know the place: a beech tree, on the grass on the right directly behind the magnificent pink entrance gate in Wilhelm-Kuhr-Strasse.

It challenges you. But it also rewards your efforts. Up there in the branches, the world is all tree. Everything else recedes far into the distance.

Everyone needs this now and again, and some people have their own special place for the purpose: their personal sanctuary, their Capri for the soul, their place for spiritual replenishment. If you are still looking for the right place, it is worth trying trees.

Children climb trees – and, something that most grown-ups can no longer conceive, they can stay up among the branches all afternoon. The forks of boughs along the trunk become whole worlds, and the tree is a universe, hidden from the eyes of adults.

In the crown of the tree you cannot help thinking about the story of little Cosimo di Ronda from the novel »Baron in the Trees«. He had to eat snails with his parents. When he refused and was ordered by his father to leave the table, he climbed defiantly into an oak tree – and stayed there 57 years.

Escape upwards – perhaps that is the impulse that lies behind the fact that tree houses are becoming more and more popular. There are now architects who have specialised in creating living space in trees. There is a trend towards searching for a place of retreat in nature, and hidden places are rare in the city – on the ground, at least. Is there anyone who never dreamed as a child of a secret hiding place, where you could simply pull up the rope ladder – and stay out of reach of everything and everyone?

Address Bürgerpark, entrance on Wilhelm-Kuhr-Strasse 9, 13187 Berlin-Pankow | Transport S2, S8, S9, U2, to Pankow (10 minutes' walk); tram M1 to Bürgerpark Pankow; bus 250, 255 to Rathaus Pankow; bus 155 to Wilhelm-Kuhr-Strasse | Tip Programme in the park: at www.pankow-feiert.de you will find the latest events in and around the Bürgerpark.

23__The Comenius Garden

A refuge with philosophical aims

The wooden gate is not very high, but closed. Those who come here for the first time stand puzzled outside the entrance and watch as people beyond it walk about under apple blossom or lie in the sun on broad benches. This place of peace and tranquillity in the middle of Neukölln seems to be inaccessible. However, it is not long before someone arrives and reveals the secret. The door opener is a small silver button. And the next time you come, you are already an initiate: the door hums, the lock opens, and you enter the confined but lush garden.

It matches the rustic idyll around it: old farmyard buildings, half-timbered houses and cobblestones. The Bohemian Village was founded here in 1737 by religious refugees – and the Comenius-Garten was laid out according to the ideas of Johann Amos Comenius, a scholar and the last bishop of the community of Bohemian Brethren. It was planned as a philosopher's and school garden – and, above all, to be open to everyone.

The theologian Comenius called for education for all, free of compulsion. In this he was far ahead of his time. All around Richardplatz, man's path through life, according to Comenius, is illustrated in several stations.

In the Comenius-Garten itself the stages in schooling that make their mark on humankind are represented. »Everything should flow from one's own impulse« is a title from his educational theory. Marvelling is the driving force for understanding – thus can Comenius be interpreted.

In this spirit, a new field of scientific research started up a few years ago in the garden of the Bohemian Village: miracle research. An extraordinary experiment by a most extraordinary group of researchers: together, children from Neukölln, scientists from the Max-Planck-Institut and artists from all over the world collect and present: miracles.

Address Richardstrasse 35, 12043 Berlin-Neukölln | **Transport** U 7 to Karl-Marx-Strasse | **Tip** Café Vux, between the Comenius-Garten and Richardplatz, has home-made cakes and gateaux, with new kinds all the time.

24__The Country House Garden
Dr Fränkel's summer seat

When the bank director Max Fränkel bought the site for his country home in around 1920, he commissioned Berlin's best landscape gardeners to plan the sloping terrain by the water. Professor Erwin Barth designed a unique themed terraced garden for him. Its clear divisions into various areas and allocation of functions is reminiscent of the ground plan of a house. By doing this the garden designer Barth was absolutely in line with the contemporary trend. In those years the »Berlin country-house movement« was entirely redefining the shaping of landscape: the idea was that nature should no longer be a prestigious but useless park. Instead it should serve the private needs of the house occupants. The garden was seen as a kind of extension of the house. And the garden in Kladow exemplifies this way of thinking.

It descends steeply to the banks of the river Havel. On the signs that have been placed on the flower-bed axis, the kitchen-garden axis, the garden pavilion and in many other places, words such as »thinning out«, »clearing away«, »wall building« and »freeing« are noticeable.

The reason for this is that the country-house garden in Kladow was in the middle of the border zone for decades, and in this period its form was almost completely lost: customs boats that patrolled on the Havel were repaired on the riverbank – and the old thatched poultry house was occupied by an angling club whose members built themselves little weekend huts all around.

But today only the information panels reveal this. It is hard to imagine that this site was not always used as a garden. Walks lead through summer meadows to the riverbank path – and at the very end a bench has been placed by the water. This bench really ought to be the 112th place in this book – because the view, the atmosphere, the old willow tree on the banks and the arch in front of the old boathouse, which still stands, make you want to write so much more.

Address Lüdickeweg 1, 14089 Berlin-Spandau | **Transport** Ferry F 10 to Alt-Kladow (10 minutes' walk); bus X 34, 134, 697 to Hottengrund | **Opening times** Mon–Thu 9am–3pm; Fri 9am–1pm; Sat, Sun and public holidays 11am–6pm | **Tip** Summer café: home-made cake is served at weekends on the terrace of the country-house garden.

25_ The Currywurst Plaque

A well-concealed memorial to Herta Heuwer,
inventor of a sauce

When you consider that the people of Berlin consume 70 million sausages in curry sauce each year and that currywurst, which was invented in 1949, has not only remained true to its origins as an honest street snack but is now served as a delicacy by top chefs, then you might well think that the woman who invented the famous curry sauce deserves some sort of fitting recognition.

On Kantstrasse you search in vain for a sign in the place where Herta Heuwer opened her snack bar in post-war Berlin, and was the first to mix a sauce made from ketchup and twelve different Indian spices and pour it over a small, sliced boiled sausage. Word of the sauce soon went round the city – and Heuwer's stand grew to become a proper little snack room which she ran along with a staff of 19 persons.

Today the building on the corner in question is an Asian supermarket. If you start your search there and walk round the building into Kaiser-Friedrich-Strasse, then you will make a discovery after all: almost on Stuttgarter Platz, a rather gloomy square next to Charlottenburg railway station, opposite sex cinemas and dimly lit pubs, there hangs a white metal sign bearing the name Herta Heuwer. Beneath, clumsily phrased and with some pathos, are the words: »Her idea is a tradition and an everlasting pleasure«. In the evening this is only visible because neon lights shine through the windows of the Asian supermarket – and the gaudy illumination above the windows proclaims: »AMAZING ORIENTAL«.

Herta Heuwer patented her invention. She is said to have revealed the recipe to nobody and finally to have taken the secret to the grave with her. Today, if you ask at a Berlin snack bar about the ingredients for their curry sauce, the answer is almost always: We're not telling! And in fact the sauce does taste a bit different everywhere you go.

Hier befand sich der Imbiss–Stand,
in dem am 4. September 1949

HERTA HEUWER

30. Juni 1913 in Königsberg – 3. Juli 1999 in Berlin

die pikante Chillup®-Sauce
für die inzwischen weltweit bekannte Currywurst erfand.

Ihre Idee ist Tradition und ewiger Genuss!

Address Kantstrasse 101/Kaiser-Friedrich-Strasse, 10627 Berlin-Charlottenburg | Transport S 7, S 9, S 75 to Charlottenburg; U 7 to Wilmersdorfer Strasse; bus M 34, X 49, 309 to Kaiser-Friedrich-Strasse/Kantstrasse; bus 109 to Charlottenburg station | Tip A Berlin currywurst: the best places for it are Konnopkes (Schönhauser Allee subway station), Curry 36 (Mehringdamm subway station) and Curry 195 (Kudamm 195).

26__ The »Degenerate Art«
Excavation

The riddle of the sculptures in the cellar

»Carry on digging!« This is what Klaus Wowereit, the mayor of Berlin, is said to have called out euphorically to the building workers in January 2010 when they found the first figure during construction work for a new subway tunnel right in front of the Rotes Rathaus (city hall). They had made a sensational find: a portrait of the actress Anni Mewes by the sculptor Edwin Scharff that was thought to have been lost. This and ten other sculptures which gradually came to light at the building site were identified as belonging to the approximately 16,000 works of art that the Nazis denounced as being »degenerate« and, for the most part, destroyed.

In the subway station Berliner Rathaus on the new line, which is intended for completion in 2014, parts of the excavation site will be visible behind glass: cellar walls from a street that existed here, Königsstrasse. Number 50, in the cellar of which all eleven sculptures were found, stood exactly opposite Berlin's city hall. By examining the way in which the works of art were lying, the archaeologists were able to deduce that they fell through burning ceilings into the cellar. This means that they were in a flat in the house.

It took more than a year to solve the riddle of the sculptures in the cellar. It was incomprehensible that banned works of art could have been in a flat opposite the city hall under National Socialist rule, as the Nazis confiscated all works that they considered incompatible with their ideas of beauty. Every tendency towards abstraction or pacifism in art was dismissed as »the art of decadence« – and forbidden.

The solution to the enigma was that Königsstrasse number 50 housed a depot of the Ministry of Propaganda, which was responsible for keeping records of censured works of art. The eleven sculptures survived the fire – but it will never be known how many works perished in the flames.

Address Rotes Rathaus, Rathausstrasse 15, 10178 Berlin-Mitte | Transport S 3, S 5, S 7, S 75; U 2, U 5, U 8; tram M 2, M 4, M 5, M 6 to Alexanderplatz station; bus M 48; 248 to Berliner Rathaus | Tip The Neues Museum: the works found on the construction site are on display on the Museumsinsel. Open Sun – Wed 10am – 6pm, Thu – Sat 10am – 8pm; tel. 030 / 266424242

27___Deko Behrendt

A cheerful place

They are called »Bushy«, »Chinese«, »Bohème« and »Flott«. They are available in black, brown, white and blond – self-adhesive false beards that cover a whole wall. Further towards the back are long shelves full of wigs, and opposite them spectacles in unusual sizes and outrageous shapes.

The quietness here is almost meditative: customers pass through worlds of colour and try on assumed identities. This is an activity at which no one wants to be disturbed. Deko Behrendt sells everything you need for fancy dress, decorations – or for a celebration. There is nothing that they don't have. And if for once something really is missing – and here everyone agrees – then you will find an alternative that is just as good.

Let's try to give an impression of the place: hanging from the ceiling are balloons, Mexican garlands, Chinese parasols, a huge inflated duck, fish, a paper cactus, lanterns, dragons and ghosts. On the shelves you will find feathery hens, sequin-covered parrots, death-heads, plastic food, cuddly balls of fabric and butterflies' wings. And then there are the motto areas: the chamber of horrors, Chinatown, the subterranean world, pirates, Mexico, animals, weddings, jubilees, the Wild West.

A shop like this can probably exist only in Berlin, a city where carnival is not celebrated. Instead of going out on the streets once a year with everyone else, the Berliners prefer to hold themed parties all year round and put on fancy dress for a variety of occasions. The wall of photos right at the back of the shop shows how many occasions you can come up with. The pictures present people in their costumes: at a barbecue party, at Christopher Street Day, on the stage – and in their living rooms. One photo shows an unhappy-looking pink rabbit on a deserted railway line, with the following words written beneath in black ink: »Thanks a lot! It's your fault I'm walking round like this!«.

Address Hauptstrasse 18, 10827 Berlin-Schöneberg | **Transport** S1 to Julius-Leber-Brücke; U7 to Kleistpark; bus M48, M85, 106 to Kaiser-Wilhelm-Platz | **Opening times** Mon–Fri 10am–7pm | **Tip** Ebbes, a shop with snacks at Crellestrasse 2: for imports from the far-away homeland of Berlin's largest immigrant community – Swabian specialities.

28__The Dining Hall of the High School for Art

Soberness versus pathos

The long room has an almost festive character. The tall windows and simple arrangement of tables and chairs elevated this student dining hall above its basic function as a canteen. At the back, wooden panelling and ceramic plates on the walls create an atmosphere almost like a living room.

The Bauhaus architect Selman Selmanagic consciously employed these effects. In the 1950s he designed new buildings for the High School of Applied Arts in Berlin-Weissensee. However, his aesthetic ideas for this extension of a former chocolate factory did not meet with the approval of the GDR culture bureaucracy. Too formalistic, not ideological enough, it was said.

Selmanagic therefore resorted to tricks. He was not allowed to build with a flat roof, for example, but in the end he constructed it so that it appears flat. He had also originally planned wide windows but, like flat roofs, these were regarded as reactionary. In the context of the great exemplary architectural project on Stalinallee, discussions about wide and high windows were held for weeks in the GDR. Finally an official decision was taken that, with reference to the Renaissance, tall windows were »more humane«. Selman Selmanagic got around this political issue by designing tall windows – but placing them one next to the other as a band of windows.

For all their soberness, the dining hall and courtyard have an intimate and protective feel. There is no longer any sign of the fact that, for many years, dialogue with social relevance was impossible here. Today the Kunsthochschule Weissensee explicitly promotes the idea that the task of art is to change the social environment through creative processes. To do so the students experiment with new forms, for example in a hitherto unique course of studies entitled »spatial strategies«.

Address Kunsthochschule Berlin-Weissensee, Bühringstrasse 20, 13086 Berlin-Weissensee | **Transport** Tram M2 to Am Steinberg; bus 156, 158, 255 to Hamburger Platz | **Tip** Exhibitions: a former department store round the corner on Hamburger Platz is used by students of the Kunsthochschule for exhibitions.

29__The Dong-Xuan-Center
Artificial flowers and fresh fish

When you push back the curtain at the entrance to the hall, you are leaving Berlin-Lichtenberg – and a moment later you are standing in the middle of a market somewhere in Asia. Here are brightly coloured artificial flowers, blinking cigarette lighters, waving cats-aromatic coriander, palettes of nail varnish, jogging pants in packets of ten or fifty, tailor-made wedding dresses and sports shoes, these too only in a pack of ten. Vietnamese music videos with lots of soft-focus effects are playing on big monitors. The atmosphere is a bizarre mixture of bustling activity and southern lassitude.

This Vietnamese world exists in the centre of Berlin, only 15 minutes from Alexanderplatz. It is called Dong Xuan – »the spring meadow« – and it blossoms in the middle of industrial wasteland in Lichtenberg.

Where power stations once pumped soot into the atmosphere, four white wholesale market halls now stand in what seems to be an endless nowhere. Colourful posters depicting Asian people glow on the façades and hoardings, but only Vietnamese-speakers can understand what they are advertising.

Some 12,000 Vietnamese live in Berlin. Most of them came as contract workers in the days of the GDR – and stayed after the Wall fell. They work, day and night, in shops selling flowers or vegetables. They are friendly, quiet and hard-working. And they stick together. You can see this in Lichtenberg: the Dong-Xuan-Center is their marketplace, not only for the purpose of shopping.

The scent of joss sticks makes the reality of Lichtenberg recede even further into the background. In the restaurants large Vietnamese families come together at long tables. In the middle of the corridor a shop-owner prays at the decorated altar next to his wares – and if you take a closer look, in between the kitsch and the special offers you will find real treasures, such as silk house-coats and old wooden carvings.

Address Herzbergstrasse 128–139, 10365 Berlin-Lichtenberg | Transport Tram M 8, 21 to Herzbergstrasse/Industriegebiet | Opening times Wed–Mon 9am–8pm; the shops in the hall have individual opening hours | Tip Pho bo, Vietnamese beef soup, is especially good and fresh in the restaurants here.

30__ Eiermann's Chapel
The hidden gem

With a single glance you take in the layout of the room. This clarity is a relief, as one moment ago you were exposed to the bustle and crowds on Breitscheidplatz. The plain rectangular space of the chapel is glazed on all sides. Beyond the windows a narrow passage leads right around it, in front of a high wall with colourful windows in a grid pattern. This design succeeds in shielding the chapel completely from life outside on the square. You look above the wall to the sky and feel you have been freed from restraints – as if the whole chapel were attached to balloons and floating above an urban chaos that never comes to rest.

Everyone knows the Gedächtniskirche. Egon Eiermann was the architect who constructed this new memorial church and its bell tower after the war around the bombed tower of the old Kaiser-Wilhelm-Kirche.

His new church with its grid of blue windows, consecrated in 1961, received a lot of praise and just as much criticism. The ruins of the old church, for their part, have been photographed by countless visitors to Berlin and sent round the world as a postcard motif. In the background, however, low, easy to miss and, in contrast to the other buildings, almost always closed, is Egon Eiermann's chapel. It is a hidden gem that few people know.

Black curtains, a simple altar, chairs with hooks on the back for bags: the architect thought of every detail. There are no distractions. Through sliding doors on either side you can step out onto the circular path, planted with bamboo.

Here all that reminds you of the city beyond the double wall is the regular, distant roaring of the subway beneath. But even this is not directly below you. There is a reason why the train drivers on Berlin's subway system speak of the »Eiermann curve«: the tunnel with the tracks had to be moved to go around the architectural ensemble of the Gedächtniskirche.

Address Breitscheidplatz, 10789 Berlin-Charlottenburg | Transport S7, S9, S75, U2, U9 to Zoologischer Garten; bus M19, M29, M46, X9, X10, X34, 100, 109, 110, 145, 200, 204, 245, various stops all around Breitscheidplatz | Opening times Daily 9am–7pm; ask in the shop in the Gedächtniskirche | Tip Der Schleusenkrug: go past Bahnhof Zoo and along the wall of the Zoologischer Garten to reach this cosy beer garden in the zoo.

31__ The Ernst-Thälmann Monument

A giant from the past

When colossal statues of Lenin were taken from their plinths in the states of eastern Europe, pictures of this were transmitted around the world and became symbols of the downfall of socialism. In Berlin, too, Lenin was one of the first to disappear from the scene. His body parts were buried in a gravel pit outside the city. After the fall of the Wall, socialist monuments were not treated kindly: the aim was to remove them as quickly as possible.

Ernst Thälmann, however, survived this period unharmed. Massive, like a giant, his imposing bust with its raised fist towers high and makes everything around it seem like an insignificant miniature.

As chairman of the German Communist Party, who was shot by the Nazis, he was posthumously assigned a special role of leadership in the GDR. The Young Pioneers made his motto their own: »Be prepared – always prepared« and swore »to live, learn and fight as Ernst Thälmann taught«.

The commission to create the bronze sculpture on Greifswalder Strasse was given to the Soviet artist Lev Yefimovich Kerbel by the government of the GDR in the 1980s. Today the massiveness of monuments in the GDR appears completely alien to us. The politician Ernst Thälmann not only has the features of his spiritual father Lenin – his figure is generalised as the archetype of the timeless revolutionary leader. The monument was stylised to such an extent that it was even controversial among East German artists. The purpose of building monuments under socialist rule was ultimately to represent communism as victorious and powerful, transcending a human scale. Today the direct political associations of the monument have receded into the background – and at a greater distance in time, this enormous Ernst Thälmann is important for future understanding of the kind of images of socialism that were held up for admiration.

Address Greifswalder Strasse, next to number 52, 10405 Berlin-Prenzlauer Berg | **Transport** S 8, S 9, S 41, S 42, S 85 to Greifswalder Strasse; tram M 4, M 10 to Greifswalder Strasse / Danziger Strasse | **Tip** The Planetarium: walk through Ernst-Thälmann-Park behind the monument towards Prenzlauer Allee to reach the Zeiss-Grossplanetarium.

32 The Fairytale Fountain
A meeting with old friends

It took twelve years until all 106 figures were in place. In 1913 the work was finally complete. The Märchenbrunnen, a superb fairytale fountain with nine jets of water spouted by frogs around the frog prince in the middle, was ceremoniously inaugurated. It was a gift from the emperor to the working-class children of Berlin. In doing so he not only donated a fountain with figures from fairy tales – he dedicated a spot in the city to them and to all the other children who came after them.

One reason why it took so many years to build the fountain was that Emperor Wilhelm II is said to have continually intervened in the planning. When everything was finally in accordance with his wishes, there was no money left: the fountain cost many times the amount that was available in the city's arts budget.

When you see the figures around the fountain and look up at them like a child, a magical world comes a little closer. Puss-in-Boots, Hansel and Gretel on two ducks, Cinderella – they are all long-standing friends.

The symbols and images from these enchanted worlds are deeply rooted within us, and have retained their status as metaphors for morality and justice. Here at the Märchenbrunnen, reason and argument lose their power. The world of magic is stronger, and not only for children.

One of the seven dwarfs surrounding Snow White is different from the others. With his lace collar and spectacles he is said to have the features of the artist Adolph Menzel. There is a conjecture about the reason for this: Emperor Wilhelm II is said to have had such a strong dislike of his realistic depictions of the tough conditions that Berlin's workers had to endure that he forbade the erection of a monument to the artist after Menzel's death. The similarity of the dwarf on Snow White's lap to Menzel is regarded as a silent protest by his artist friends against the emperor's prohibition.

Address Friedenstrasse/Am Friedrichshain, 10249 Berlin-Friedrichshain | Transport Tram M 4, bus 142, 200 to Am Friedrichshain | Opening times The park is closed at night. | Tip Freiluftkino Friedrichshain: open-air cinema in the summer – and you can even take your own barbecue.

33__ The Former Prison
A place with a history – and a future

The poplars on the bank are densely planted. In summer they make it impossible to look through from the other side of the bay. In winter, however, it is easy to see what for a long time was intended to remain out of sight: the old brick buildings of Rummelsburg, a former East German prison. Today new black-and-white buildings glimmer through the bare branches, then the red prison façade, and above the tips of the ramrod-straight trees a crane reaches for the sky. The wall around the prison has disappeared, and behind it new paving stones lead across recently levelled ground. Trees have been planted next to the path.

The six brick buildings, which date from 1880 and are protected monuments, have been given a facelift. »BerlinCampus« is the name of this housing estate in Rummelsburg Bay. Cells on long corridors have been turned into exclusive apartments. Nothing more serves as a reminder that the Nazis once interned homosexuals and »mental deviants« here, and that under the GDR government six prisoners had to share an area of 14 square metres. The aura of power that surrounds these buildings is still perceptible – but the feeling of foreboding disappears as soon as you see how new life has been breathed into the site: fresh mortar in the joints, balconies and little gardens with children's toys imbue these bulky anonymous blocks with a human air that would once have seemed impossible.

In other cities, too, deserted prisons have become sought-after pieces of real estate, though of a different kind: in Stockholm you can spend the night in former cells on the Langholmen Peninsula. In Oxford a design hotel with prison ambience was created in buildings dating back to the 10th century. Tourism with a spine-chilling touch has actually been proclaimed a trend in the travel business. Sometime in the future, nothing in Rummelsburg will act as a reminder of the prison. Times change, but what remains is a place with its own special history.

Address Berlin Campus, Karl-Wilker-Strasse, 10317 Berlin-Lichtenberg | **Transport** S 3 to Rummelsburg (10 minutes' walk); tram 21 to Kosanke Siedlung | **Tip** An unusual guided tour: Cliewe Juritza, who was once imprisoned in Rummelsburg on »suspicion of attempting to cross the border«, gives tours of the site today – tel. 0179 / 4729007.

34 __ Good Wedding, Bad Wedding

»Mitte is schitte«

Longish black hair combed back with gel, a thick gold chain over his black shirt – this is Murat in the ticket booth as he greets each guest with a handshake. Normally he works in Uncle Ahmed's kebab shop. A moment later the ticket booth and Murat have disappeared, and he is on stage in the theatre: »Welcome to Prime Time.«

The auditorium is full, as it is every evening when the latest episode of the theatre soap »Good Wedding, Bad Wedding« is staged in the Prime Time Theater. Before it begins there is a summary of the story so far, during which the series song is played: »Mitte is schitte. Prenzelberg is petting. Real sex is only Wedding«. (For the uninitiated: Mitte is the city centre, Prenzelberg is posh, and Wedding is a workers' quarter). Then, with lots of wigs, noise and exquisitely biting satire, we are in the thick of it: Katrin, a pupil at a caring, spiritual Waldorf school, wants to do something for her karma by helping others. Where do people need help? In Wedding, of course. The people of Wedding are happy to be helped, so Katrin first sorts bills in Uncle Ahmed's kebab shop and delivers letters for postman Kalle, so he can watch the second half of the football match. »Out of their minds, the Prenzelers«, says Kalle, shaking his shock of hair at good-girl Katrin.

Since the first episode in 2004, the series has revolved around the unbridgeable gap between down-to-earth Wedding and the head-in-the-clouds Prenzelbergers who live on the other side of the »wicked bridge«. Newcomers to the series are Friedrichhainis, who play the guitar with flowing, uncombed locks and speak with so many subordinate clauses and subjunctives that they can't make it to the end of a sentence. When you go home after an evening here, you feel really good – because Murat, Uncle Ahmed, Kalle and Katrin will be back in the next episode. Must be continued!

Address Prime Time Theater, Müllerstrasse 163 (entrance on Burgsdorfstrasse), 13353 Berlin-Wedding | **Transport** S 41, S 42, U 6 to Wedding; bus 120 to Gerichtstrasse | **Opening times** Information: tel. 030/49907958 or www.primetimetheater.de | **Tip** Buy a mobile phone: when you present a ticket for the Prime Time Theater – according to the notice at the theatre entrance – you get 10 per cent off the price of all mobiles at Elektro & Kiosk at Müllerstrasse 164.

35__ The Graffiti »Periferia Connection«

New perspectives at »Pro social«

The back wall of the garage is a story with a happy end. Young people from Paris, Rome and Berlin have told this story, which is their own. They came from the high-rises of the Cité Pablo Picasso, Bella Monaca and Marzahn, stayed for a week in the »Pro social« house, got to know Berlin – and did some spraying. The title of their graffiti is »Periferia Connection«. The mummified youth who can be seen on the painting has been locked up. Behind him you can make out the skyline of Roman suburbs. The kids who grow up here hardly ever leave their own neighbourhood. They don't get to know other countries or cultures. They are imprisoned within the social conditions in which they were brought up. In the second part of this painted story, which is taller than a man, many different keys are lying on the ground. In the background, the circular tower blocks of suburbs in Paris rise to the sky. And then, on the roughly plastered back wall of the garage, everything turns out well: the key fits, the door opens – and all at once many opportunities arise. These are symbolised by an aircraft, a Berlin train and a ship. The world is no longer something abstract outside their own estate – it is open.

Of course, things look different in reality. But the not-for-profit housing association here in Marzahn makes efforts to give young people from a difficult social background the chance to get to know new surroundings and meet others of their own age.

The unimpressive concrete block is not only used for meetings of young people, but also for something else that makes the »Pro social« project unique: since 1998 tourists, homeless persons and asylum seekers have stayed here under one roof. The guests in the two halves of the house, both in the hostel for homeless and in the tourist guesthouse, have one thing in common: Marzahn provides most of them with a new perspective.

Address Blumberger Damm 12, 12683 Berlin-Marzahn | Transport Bus X 69, 154, 191, 291 to Cecilienstrasse/Blumberger Damm | Opening times See www.pro-social.de | Tip The Marzahn windmill: surrounded by concrete towers, one of Berlin's last remaining windmills is in operation in the centre of Alt-Marzahn, at Hinter der Mühle 4.

36 __ The Graphothek
Art for all

A new picture on the wall always catches the eye. At first. But usually it is not long before you get used to the sight. The pictures sink into old, familiar surroundings. Some guests notice that it is new – but sooner or later nobody talks about it, and nobody takes a close look at it any more.

That is the moment when you should swap it for a new picture. This is possible in the Graphothek in the Märkisches Viertel district, which loans art as libraries lend books. Pictures that otherwise can only be seen in museums or private collections hang on the wall here in files that you can leaf through. And this is just a fraction of the total. Most of the works, 5000 of them altogether, are stored in countless drawers.

At the counter the pictures are framed, packed and tied up with bands of fabric. Then off they go to the next exhibition site – a living room, a medical practice or an office somewhere in Berlin. It costs five euros to rent a picture for three months, and by paying 25 euros for an annual subscription you can borrow three pictures and exchange them as often as you like.

Since 1968 the Graphothek, the first institution of its kind in Germany, has been lending out art, and has built up a considerable collection since it first opened. For some artists there are long waiting lists, and works by Marc Chagall and Franz Marc, for example, are almost always on display somewhere.

The location of the Graphothek, the public library in the Märkisches Viertel, is important for the way it sees its work. It aims to provide access to art, above all for people who do not go to museums to look at paintings, photography or prints. And this surely corresponds to the artists' wishes. A work does not remain in the possession of a single person. Instead the pictures are experienced anew again and again, and accompany different people for a while on their way through life.

Address Stadtteilbibliothek, Königshorster Strasse 6, 13439 Berlin-Reinickendorf | Transport S1, U8 to Wittenau; bus M21, X21, X33, 122, 124, 221, 321 to Königshorster Strasse | Opening times Mon 3–7pm, Tue 1–5pm, Thu 3–7pm, Fri 11am–5pm, closed Wed | Tip Galerie M: art from and about Marzahn – studios in Marzahn regularly exhibit their work here: Marzahner Promenade 13, near Marzahn station.

37__Greenwich Promenade

Where time stands still

Everything fits together perfectly, creating a scene that looks like a promenade in a park in a Mediterranean spa: plane trees on the bank, 1960s restaurants with spacious terraces by the lake – and of course the pier for steamers.

Nevertheless, you don't quite believe your eyes: on the Tegeler See time seems to have stood still at some moment between the 1970s and the 1980s. You walk along the banks of this lake almost cautiously so as not to burst this bubble of tranquillity and prevent a piece of Berlin from being sucked into the whirlwind pace of world events. No one would be surprised if a scoop of ice cream still cost 80 pfennigs here.

And then you are presented with the icing on the cake: you rarely get to hear »Berliner Schnauze«, the big mouth that the locals are famous for, in a ruder, brasher or more authentic form. Leisure activities on the Tegeler See, consisting of crazy golf and pedalo hire, are directed by a unique duo from a small log cabin at the end of the promenade. It is worth stopping and observing this double act, which they have been practising for so long that they now identify with their roles perfectly.

They don't really want to be included in a book about 111 Places in Berlin, but never mind, they have appeared in a lot of books already. Crazy golf has been on offer here since 1950 and boat hire since 1900. If you want to know more, go to the local museum. During this conversation they shout instructions to the people in the pedaloes.

The comments are not for sensitive souls. Anyone who mixes up left and right while pedalling backwards gets a thorough telling-off, but nobody here bothers too much. This tone of voice is part of the atmosphere of an excursion to the Tegeler See. On the water a swan waits for the next trip with its head held high. Is this a popular boat? The stock answer is: well, with lovers, yes.

Address Greenwich-Promenade on the Tegeler See, 13507 Berlin-Reinickendorf | **Transport** S 25 to Tegel; U 6 to Alt-Tegel; bus 124, 133, 222 to An der Mühle (10–15 minutes' walk in each case) | **Opening times** Boat hire and crazy golf daily 10am–7pm | **Tip** Moby-Dick: a whale-shaped steamer with sharks' teeth to match the 1980s scene sails down the Havel to Wannsee.

38_ Grunewald Hunting Lodge
Unbridled pleasures behind the walls

When the woods around Grunewald lake were still a marshy area outside the city walls, there were no joggers here, not even people out for a walk. Grunewald was not only difficult to reach – until 1904 it was a royal hunting ground. Jagdschloss Grunewald, the hunting lodge that Elector Joachim II built in 1542, was completely secluded. It was also empty most of the time.

The great gate in the wall was only opened for guests occasionally in winter. And then it was time for hunting. And for festivities. Today, when you stand in front of the fireplace in the hall, surrounded by walls metres thick, then it's easy to imagine that, away from Wilhelmine etiquette, the celebrations were not the same as at court.

A wild boar of white porcelain occupies the middle of the table. It has been here since 1860. No one knows what goings-on in front of the fireplace its opaque white eyes have seen, but recently letters were discovered that report of extremely licentious parties in the hunting lodge in Wilhelm II's reign.

The anonymous letters of denunciation, addressed to the party guests themselves as well as other members of court, describe in great detail an orgy that took place in the winter of 1891. The emperor himself was not implicated in the scandal, but 15 members of his court were alleged to have taken their pleasure here behind the thick walls after a sleigh ride.

It proved impossible to discover the name of the author of the letters, although the persons involved did everything they could to preserve their reputations and employed a host of aristocratic amateur detectives to expose the wagging tongue in their ranks. On this occasion the thick walls of Jagdschloss Grunewald were not sufficient protection – the newspapers and the public took a merciless interest in the scandal.

Since then the little hunting lodge in the Grunewald forest has lost its good name.

Address Hüttenweg 100 (on Grunewaldsee), 14193 Berlin-Zehlendorf | Transport Bus X10, X83, 115 to Königin-Luise-Strasse/Clayallee (15 minutes' walk through the woods) | Opening times April–Oct Tue–Sun 10am–6pm, Nov–March Sat–Sun and public holidays only with a guided tour at 11am, 1pm and 3pm, closed 1 April–10 June | Tip Spend the night in the lodge: if you are not afraid of the resident ghost of Anna Sydow, reserve a room – the only one – in the courtyard buildings. Tel: 030/8181910.

39__The Hafenkirche

The church of Berlin's last boatmen's pastor

Hardly any ships moor here nowadays. The harbour basin lies in ghostly silence, surrounded by huge warehouses with façades of dark brick. When the boatmen's pastor Fedor Pfistner heads for the harbour in the evening in his church boat, it is often the only vessel. The Lutheran Church has decided not to make a new appointment to the job, as the number of believers among the boatmen has declined. However, Fedor Pfistner carries on as before.

As the last pastor in this job he still feels a responsibility towards the boatmen, and so he travels the canals, locks and lakes with his little church boat.

The church in the harbour, the Westhafen, had to move. It is no longer easy to find, and even the gate porter had to look for it on the map.

It is now accommodated in a small, multi-purpose room containing an altar with candles and ships' lamps, a baptismal font welded to a four-pronged anchor – and of course a model of the Berlin church ship WICHERN ARCHE NOVA, built in 1904. All that remains of the old Arche Nova is a large white cross with the ship's bell. It is leaning against the wall in the entrance hall between piled-up crates, as a proper place for it has not yet been found.

»Advice + help« is the short but clear message at the entrance to the harbour church. However, the duties of the boatmen's pastor also include going out to the people who need his help.

It is a proper mission, says Fedor Pfistner. Once a week he sails off – although he has a new job as a student pastor – in the new WICHERN ARCHE NOVA, an elegant, sporty boat with mahogany sides. He makes contact with the boatmen by radio, talks to them and holds services at captains' meetings in the region.

A blue flag with a white anchor that merges into a cross flies from his boat. The anchor cross is one of many symbols that everyone recognises on the waterways.

Address Westhafenstrasse 1, 13353 Berlin-Wedding | **Transport** S 41, S 42, U 9 to Westhafen | **Opening times** By arrangement only: e-mail HsSchiffB@aol.com or tel. 030/ 39879119 | **Tip** The newspaper archive of the Staatsbibliothek: in the reading room of the state library, a converted grain warehouse, you can look across the harbour through portholes while reading newspapers from all over the world. Opening times: Mon – Fri 9am – 5pm, Sat 9am – 1pm.

40_ The Hannah-Höch-Garten
A bequest with a meaning

The painter and her garden were one. When Hannah Höch, an influential artist with a determining role in Berlin's Dadaist movement, was awarded an honorary professorship by the Academy of Arts, she said to her friends: »My garden will be pleased about that. Now leave me alone with the souls of my flowers. I want to share this pleasure with them alone.« She had a deep relationship with each and every plant around her little wooden house with its pale blue window shutters. Each flower, each lavender bush, the strange and enticing dittany that she brought back herself from her journey on foot to Italy, and the old fruit trees – everything here had its place in the greater whole.

Peter Carlberg, Hannah Höch's nephew, described this closeness from his own point of view: »Hannah Höch was my aunt – and no garden anywhere is as much my uncle as this one.«

The artist sketched her flower beds in a garden book and wrote down her thoughts about them. These are the kind of interconnections which she thought out exactly and which today still make the garden so full of life. There are also flowing transitions between the house and the garden.

On the veranda climbing plants are in bloom up to the ceiling, and doors are wide open on every side of the house. It is as if the garden were flooding the interior of the house.

Hannah Höch wanted to blur the fixed boundaries that people wish to draw around everything that can be achieved. In order to understand her paintings and collages, you have to let her garden work on you.

And this contact will be maintained. She ensured this herself by bequeathing the garden to the district government after her death – with one condition attached: the house may only be let to artists who keep and care for the spirit of the garden and open it for everybody at least once a year.

Address An der Wildbahn 33, 13503 Berlin-Reinickendorf | Transport S25 to Schulzen-
dorf (15 minutes' walk); bus 133 to Bekassinenweg | Opening times Viewing by arrange-
ment only, tel. 030/4314824 | Tip Haus Dannenberg, Alt-Heiligensee 52 – 54: this country
restaurant by a lake was Hannah Höch's favourite place to eat out.

41__ The Hansaviertel
The spirit of a new beginning

In the middle of the Tiergarten district, ten minutes from Potsdamer Platz and ten minutes from the zoo, you suddenly find yourself in a model town. It is not a miniature, however, but consists of real family homes, high-rises, pavilions and gardens – designed by a total of 36 international architects.

The Hansaviertel was the heart of the international building exhibition INTERBAU 1957 in Berlin. It was about making dreams of modern life come true. Children were told at the time: this is how they live in countries like Sweden or France. Visitors took a chair lift across the construction site from the Zoologischer Garten to Bellevue – and felt proud.

Today the model quarter is a scene of village peace and seclusion. High-rises next to detached houses next to multi-party houses next to bungalows – what these diverse homes have in common is a love of form and clarity.

At Händelallee 33–39 the Danish architect Arne Jacobsen designed a four-family house for the exhibition. A birch with two trunks spreads its branches protectively over the low, single-storey building. Its north side facing the street has no windows. You guess that at the back this elongated U-shape opens to the light. From the moment when the four families step out of the front door onto the street, they go their own way – but in the living area at the back they are together. This was the innovation in Jacobsen's architecture: in houses accommodating several families, he replaced unconnected parallel living with a common focal point.

Big ideas for a new, social way of living in the future can be found here next door to each other. But little remains of this spirit of a new beginning. The arcade of shops on Hansaplatz looks down-at-heel, seems almost to have died out. St Ansgar's Church has closed, and in the Berlin Pavilion of INTERBAU it smells of frying fat – Burger King has moved in.

Address Händelallee 33–39, 10557 Berlin-Tiergarten | **Transport** S 3, S 5 to Tiergarten; U 9 to Hansaplatz; bus 106 to Hansaplatz subway station | **Tip** Houseboats: opposite the Berlin Pavilion, on the other side of Strasse des 17. Juni, residents of houseboats live in idyllic surroundings on a small stretch of canal.

42__ The Hasenschänke
United in leisure

The Hasenheide (the name means »rabbit heath«) has a bad reputation. Perhaps rightly so. But when you come from the Kreuzberg side and have done the steep ascent, you immediately feel liberated. As if you had shaken off the streets, noise and commotion. There are fewer drug dealers, too. You pass the crazy golf and the petting zoo. The playground is on the left, and on the right the blue seats of the open-air cinema shine through the bushes – and then you have reached the real heart of the Hasenheide: the Hasenschänke.

With its kidney-shaped concrete roof and paved area in front, it looks like a 1950s petrol station. At the exact centre of the building, disproportionately small and looking a bit lost, a café peeps out: the Hasenschänke. Only a kiosk, some people think, and turn away disappointed. But it is worthwhile stopping here and doing what the others do: switch off and don't bother too much about anything. At lots of round tables with blue plastic chairs, you can observe a unique phenomenon.

In good weather everyone mingles here to form one mass of leisure-seekers: regular guests from Neukölln, young parents from Kreuzberg, genteel Tempelhofers taking a walk, even people doing sports – all in an extremely good mood.

For 15 years the Schneider family have been running this Neukölln snack bar, which was built in 1950. They serve sausages, meatballs and potato salad. Or cake, ice cream and chocolate bars. The guests stick to their gender roles: she has a cup of coffee, he drinks beer from the bottle. At the next table a pack of cards has appeared. After the second beer at the latest you get into conversation with the people around.

This place, surrounded by old trees, never fails to impress: for the space of an afternoon it succeeds in suspending social conventions. Everything is subordinated to the common purpose of general relaxation and recreation.

Address Volkspark Hasenheide, south of the cemetery, 10965 Berlin-Neukölln | Transport U7 to Südstern; bus 140 to Fichtestrasse | **Opening times** 1 March–31 Oct daily 10am–midnight, on winter weekends 11am–6pm | **Tip** Karstadt on Hermannplatz: the department store which was built here in 1929 and destroyed in the war was said to have been the most impressive in Europe. There is a model of it on the upper floor of the Karstadt store that now stands here.

43___Heimathafen Neukölln

A new kind of popular theatre

People wanted to be entertained – and here they found entertainment. Of every imaginable kind. That was back in the days when Neukölln was still called Rixdorf. »I'm looking forward to Sunday / Then we'll go out there / ... There's music in Rixdorf ...« to quote the words of a well-known old hit. This was not just a popular song, but a way of life. At weekends people went out there to celebrate. And their wishes were met in Rixdorf: countless dance halls, ballrooms and shady establishments sprang up here outside the city. One place that opened was Niesigks Salon, a ballroom that quickly became an institution for pleasure-hungry city dwellers.

Eventually, in 1912, the tumultuous goings-on to the south-west of the city reached the stage where Rixdorf was renamed Neukölln – so that the area could recover from its completely ruined reputation.

Today this district again has to fight its bad image. For the ten founders of Heimathafen Neukölln (meaning »home port«) in 2009, precisely this was the reason to start up a theatre in Neukölln. It was the ideal place for fulfilling their vision of a new popular theatre in Berlin.

The programme in the old Niesigks Salon is just as colourfully mixed today as it was in the Rixdorf days – and as varied as Neukölln is today: plays, variety shows, poetry slams, concerts, parties, boxing matches and fashion shows.

Heimathafen Neukölln does not see itself only as a place of entertainment, however: the group who run it want to develop a new kind of theatre, close to the people, in Neukölln.

With »Arabboy« and »Arabqueen«, Heimathafen Neukölln was one of the first theatres to deal with the subject of the way young Muslims feel in Germany. These two plays in the »Neukölln Trilogy« based on novels by Güner Balci are not intended to preach but to give encouragement and reach out to people, in Neukölln and elsewhere.

Address Karl-Marx-Strasse 141, 12043 Berlin-Neukölln | Transport U 7 to Karl-Marx-Strasse | Opening times Information: tel. 030/56821333 or www.heimathafen-neukoelln.de | Tip Körnerpark: between Schierkerstrasse and Jonasstrasse lies a Baroque park in the middle of a residential area, with cascades, an orangery, fountains and a gallery for changing exhibitions.

44__ The house where David Bowie lived

Heroes in a two-room flat in Schöneberg

The house stands halfway up a slope. That's unusual in Berlin. But otherwise this is an average-looking old multi-party house painted a dreary grey-white-yellow. An Indian restaurant, a car-hire office, a tattoo parlour and a medical practice are crowded together on the ground floor. Between them is the front door. In 1976 David Bowie went through this door, in Hauptstrasse 155, and decided to move into a two-room flat on the first floor. His neighbour in the house was called Iggy Pop.

When Bowie came to Berlin he was finished, it is said. Wrecked by drugs. In Berlin he is supposed to have got back on his feet again. He came here in order to make recordings – and stayed three years. His albums »Low« and »Heroes« were recorded at Hansa Studios, and he also did a few songs in Berlin with Iggy Pop.

Two houses further along, at Hauptstrasse 157, the owners of the bar called Neues Ufer have placed tables and chairs out on the pavement. In David Bowie's day the name of the place was Anderes Ufer, and it acted as a second living room for the musicians from number 155: they came for their breakfast, and to drink whisky in the evenings. It was the first openly gay and lesbian café in Schöneberg that you could look inside and where everyone could simply walk in without pressing a bell or any kind of secrecy. On one occasion the window was smashed, and David Bowie is said to have paid for a new pane of glass. They no longer know what kind of whisky he drank here, but it is said that when he is in Berlin, Bowie always has himself driven past the house in Hauptstrasse. »A city full of bars for sad, disappointed people. I love that«, David Bowie once said about the city. And they love him in Berlin. The proof is that time and again fans remove the sign bearing the house number 155 and take it away as a memento of his life.

Address Hauptstrasse 155, 10827 Berlin-Schöneberg | Transport U7 to Kleistpark; bus M85, M48, 106, 187, 204 to Kleistpark subway station | Tip Listen to music: two blocks away at Kolonnenstrasse 64 you can browse for music in the JAKSCH record shop.

45__ The Hüttenpalast

A place for everyone

Indoors is outdoors here. This large factory hall in a back yard in Neukölln is a campsite all year round.

Every morning a bag of bread rolls hangs on the doors of the caravans, and thermos flasks of coffee are placed beneath birch trees in the middle.

Summer or winter, all the guests can take their breakfast at camping tables uncombed and wearing flip-flops, and run an eye over their neighbours before they dress up for the city and go out onto the street through the café in the building at the front.

The Hüttenpalast (»palace of huts«) is more than a nice place to stay: artists from the neighbourhood exhibit their pictures, design whole guest rooms or give concerts in the yard. The two women who founded the Hüttenpalast were not primarily interested in setting up a profitable business, but in doing something creative in their local area. They wanted to try out something of their own.

That is why anything is possible – a situation that matches the way of life here between Sonnenallee and Maybachufer. Artists and freelancers gradually moved to the northern part of Neukölln, taking advantage of low rents to occupy the numerous little shops that had been empty for a long time and had once been bakeries and corner shops for the area.

To understand the phenomenon of gentrification, it helps to walk round the streets here: little workshops, pubs in living rooms and shared offices are busily setting up – at an incredible pace. Neukölln has long ceased to be a secret for insiders, and is now a fashionable quarter.

It is to be hoped that the attractive factory yards with their old Berlin charm don't fall into the hands of property speculators, but that the locals form networks and support each other, as here in the Hüttenpalast – and so keep some of the authentic character that makes the neighbourhood so lively at the moment.

Address Hobrechtstrasse 65/66, 12047 Berlin-Neukölln | Transport U7, U8 to Hermannplatz; bus M29, 171, 194, 344 to Hermannplatz/Sonnenallee subway station | Opening times Information: tel. 030/37305806 or www.huettenpalast.de | Tip »Ä«: this corner pub with flowery armchairs and living-room lamps at Weserstrasse 40 may no longer be a secret, but it is a Neukölln institution.

46__Hut Town
Just like a real town …

The sound of hammering rises and falls ceaselessly across the Panke Valley. If you walk towards the banging, you see wooden boards. Long and short boards, thick and thin boards, and boards on which you can read old imprints and stamps. And then you see what results from all these boards together: roofs, steps, huts and a castle in the middle with an impressive bridge linking the towers. Not a day goes by without the sound of hammering here. Every day the town of huts at Pinke-Panke children's farm grows a little more, in an unforeseeable and unplanned way.

When there is no space left the old huts are pulled down again – just like in a real town. Only the big castle in the middle remains. It is the community house, where all the children are allowed to join in the building work. The smaller huts around it are usually under construction – supervised and carried out by architectural teams or individual architects.

As soon as the framework with posts is a stable structure, there are no limits to what you can do in Hut Town. You can take inspiration from the buildings around you: there are little towers, bridges to the house next door and terraces. Even a wooden car was knocked together here recently.

When you have found your way through the narrow alleyways of the town, past the entrances through which you can look inside this world of wooden boards, you reach the caravan where tools are handed out. Nobody here checks up on how you build, but only on what you use to build it: everyone who gets a saw, a hammer and nails is entered into a thick ledger.

Girls and boys usually set to work separately in Hut Town. While the girls generally prefer to continue work on a house that has been started and to install little benches and tables, the boys, by contrast, often start by pulling down all that exists of an old hut, and then design a new one starting from scratch.

Address Kinderbauernhof Pinke-Panke, Am Bürgerpark 15 – 18, 13156 Berlin-Pankow |
Transport S 1, S 25, S 85 to Wollankstrasse; bus 250 to the continuation of Koloniestrasse |
Opening times Tue – Fri noon – 6pm (Nov – March until 5.30pm), Sat, Sun and public holi-
days 10am – 6pm (Nov – March until 5.30pm), closed Monday | **Tip** Felt-making, carving
or pottery: the workshops at Pinke Panke children's farm are open for everybody free of
charge. www.kinderbauernhof-pinke-panke.de

47__Intershop 2000
The history collector's treasures

»Ostalgia« – nostalgia for the days of East Germany – long ago ceased to be an insignificant niche. The marketing of »holy relics« or other items connected with the GDR is booming in Berlin. It is no surprise to find large- and small-scale replicas, but the range of newly invented products is astounding: pasta in the shape of the »Ampelmännchen« (the traffic-light figure), »Hero of Labour« shower gel or condoms inscribed »Be prepared, always prepared«, not to mention the countless T-shirts with mottos such as »Ossis do it better«.

Intershop 2000 stocks none of this. In a small district north of Stralauer Allee, like an island separated from the rest of the city by the Spree and the railway tracks, genuine treasures from days gone by are heaped up in a former Konsum shop.

Elke Matz has gathered them together. It happened in an unplanned way. She liked the crockery used for railway catering, and in 1990 went off to look for it, collecting cups, saucers, plates and milk jugs in countless station cafés between Hof and Rostock before they were thrown away. Today, over 20 years later, the shelves are creaking under piles of crockery.

It's not only porcelain that has survived here. You can browse through and buy toys, books, original posters for peace and many more relics of the GDR.

And Elke Matz has not only collected them – the items and their histories find their way to her. Still today. People know that the Intershop is a good place for their things, and they bring them in.

Some Eastern products have kept going after the fall of the Wall and still have a role, not only in places devoted to Ostalgia. For example the egg-cups with a chicken, made by Sonja PLASTIC near Chemnitz. Everyone who grew up in the GDR knows these colourful plastic chickens. This is one of the stories that you can learn about in Intershop 2000 – a success story.

Address Dannecke Strasse 8, 10245 Berlin-Friedrichshain | **Transport** S 3, S 5, S 7, S 75, U 1 to Warschauer Strasse; bus 347 to Lahmbruckstrasse | **Opening times** Wed−Fri 2−6pm, Sat−Sun 12−6pm | **Tip** The Zwingli-Kirche: no services are held now in this church, but you can view exhibitions there, at Rotherstrasse 3.

48__ The Island in the Carp Pond

Directions for explorers

The island is a place that you have to track down. It would be un-satisfactory to explain where it lies, what it looks like and what is to be found there − everyone has to find and explore it for themselves. What gives this place its character is wandering through the Trep-tower Park and finally having the feeling of chancing on something special.

The following directions will help you to search for the small hid-den island in the carp pond. On the side of the Treptower Park near to the river Spree there is a weekend and day-trip atmosphere every day − steamers put in at the jetty, there are fish rolls to eat and ped-aloes to hire.

If you leave the river bank and walk into the park, it gets quieter. There is so much space on the grass between the old trees that it never becomes too crowded. Further back in the park stands the mas-sive Soviet monument. On the other side of the war graves, a little bit concealed behind the trees, lies the carp pond.

It is not a big lake − but all the same, it's larger than other ponds in city parks. A little trodden-out path winds through the bushes along the bank. If you follow it, you walk bent and unseen as if on a Red Indian track, but you won't lose the way, as it always follows the shore. And when you are almost ready to give up, because you have walked nearly all the way round the lake − all at once, just beyond the bridge, you see an island. From the other side and from the water it is not recognisable as an island, as it lies only a short distance, per-haps four or five metres, from the bank. There is no bridge, but the water is not deep here. Three or four slender tree trunks provide a temporary and extremely wobbly way from one bank to the other. And if you really want to stay on the island undisturbed for a while, all you have to do is raise the tree trunks …

Address In the Treptower Park, by the sycamore tree with the following number on its sign: 1009 9, 12435 Berlin-Treptow | **Transport** S 8, S 9, S 85 to Plänterwald; bus 166, 265 to Klingerstrasse | **Tip** The Archenhold Observatory: from Treptower Park the world's longest telescope, on the roof of the observatory (Alt-Treptow 1), is visible.

49_ The Jewish Cemetery
Eternal remembrance

»What we preserve in coffins / belongs to time. / What we love, remains, / and remains for ever.« The letters of this inscription shine brightly on the black polished stone. When you move on, the words remain in your mind – and provide an explanation for this place. Beneath tall trees the gravestones have been placed close together. Some of them have toppled into the carpet of ivy or are held up only by the stone next to them. Nobody can now pass through the narrow paths between the graves. In Jewish cemeteries the deceased are given over to eternity – and to the community.

In the Jewish cemetery there are also signs that the dead are remembered here, on the spot. Little piles of stones lie on the gravestones. They are in all shapes and colours, and were brought here from many places.

There are a number of different explanations for this ritual. It is certainly an appropriate gesture to leave behind something that endures for ever. A stone is something unimaginable and infinite – a memento placed there for all eternity.

All are equal in death. At Jewish cemeteries you can get used to this thought: usually all the gravestones are equally plain and of the same size. It is unusual here in Weissensee that a number of magnificent funeral monuments, often in a state of decay, stand out from the wild, jungle-like undergrowth. The reason for this is that in the time of Emperors Wilhelm I and II, when many Christians built splendid tombs for themselves, the fashion caught on among wealthy Jews too.

In the Nazi period the cemetery was not destroyed, and not even closed. However, this period left its mark, of course, as can be seen on many gravestones with spaces that remained empty.

The cemetery in Weissensee tells of Jewish history that is also the history of Berlin and Germany – and is not yet a closed chapter.

Address Herbert-Baum-Strasse 45, 13088 Berlin-Weissensee | Transport Tram M 4, M 13, 12 to Albertinenstrasse; bus 156 to Michelangelostrasse | Opening times Mon–Thu 7.30am–5pm (in winter until 4pm); Fri 7.30am–2.30pm; Sun 8–5pm (in winter until 4pm); closed Sat and on public holidays | Tip The Jüdisches Museum: the Jewish Museum presents permanent exhibitions and German-Jewish history from the point of view of the Jewish minority. Lindenstrasse 9am–2pm. Opening times: Mon 10am–10pm, Tue–Sun: 10am–8pm

50__ The Juke Box

A trusty companion

It's nice when you find that things simply don't change. In a city that is always moving ahead, getting faster and faster, mercilessly and at an intolerable pace, everyone needs places that stay just as they are and provide something to lean on in this whirlwind of change.

You can rely on the juke box in the Ankerklause. It has always had its place opposite the bar counter – and it will remain there. Everyone has to walk past it.

During daylight hours you pass it to go out onto the terrace, where bright red geraniums send signals of cosy warmth across the Landwehrkanal. When it gets dark, and until the early hours, the wide juke box with its mirrors is queen of the night, here by the water. It is always at the heart of the action.

The pub is always crowded – but sooner or later in the course of an evening, the moment arrives when the spot in front of the juke box unexpectedly becomes free – and without anything special in mind, suddenly you are standing there yourself and pushing the buttons with arrows on four CD cases. Every click brings a tingling of anticipation – and already the next two CDs are making their way to the top with a little jolt.

It is always worthwhile celebrating nostalgia. It is present here, in the covers that you click through like the soundtrack of your own life, and in an unpredictable mixture of blues, rock 'n' roll and electronic music that you cannot hear in any club in the whole world but, if it is to be found anywhere, exists only on dusty cassettes somewhere in your cupboard as a memory of your favourites list from the old days.

The true intimates of the juke box can be recognised by the fact that they ignore the arrow buttons and type in the four-digit combinations of the songs without even looking.

And if you can't decide, on this juke box you can always rely on the current top ten.

Address Kottbusser Damm 104, 10967 Berlin-Kreuzberg | Transport U 8 to Schönlein-strasse | Opening times Daily from 10am | Tip Party without the juke box: every Thursday a DJ makes the music in the Ankerklause: not much space, lots of people and a really good atmosphere.

51 Karl-Marx-Allee

Slow process of change

It lies there like a stranded space ship – gigantic, overpowering, with no link to the outside world. On its show side, towards Alexanderplatz, new porcelain shines on the old workers' palaces – but further out of the city, the façades of this great avenue become darker and the splendour starts to crumble.

The whole colossus seems like a picturesque and magnificent stage-set for socialism. A piece of Moscow. And it seems as if the power of the past is keeping hold of this showcase street and preventing it from linking up to present-day Berlin – and finding a new place for itself in the city.

Like a metaphor for this state of hovering between yesterday and today, neon letters from the old days are lit above the shop in number 78–84: the Karl Marx Bookshop was an institution, in both East and West. Here, alongside Marx and Mao, you also found the works of Thomas Mann, Christa Wolf and Bertolt Brecht.

Today there are no more books to be seen through the shop window, and no antiques are piled up beneath the fine round arches. In 2008, after 55 years, the bookshop had to move out, as the rent in the refurbished Block C South had become too expensive.

Having books in this place was once part of a bigger plan: the bookshop with a surface of 1500 square metres was intended to demonstrate – especially to the West – the great importance of literature in the GDR.

What was originally called Stalin-Allee was the primary image project of the GDR government. It is the story of rebuilding from the rubble, of a workers' revolt on the huge construction site, and above all of a massive project in a uniform style: Stalin-Allee was planned down to the last detail, from the subway station to the street lamps, from the cinema to every last mosaic. The present day has yet to find a purpose for a street that was once forced through as a single huge scheme.

Address Karl-Marx-Allee, 10178 Berlin-Friedrichshain | **Transport** U5 to Strausberger Platz; bus 142 to Strausberger Platz subway station | **Tip** Audio-tour: on a walk along Karl-Marx-Allee you meet a construction worker and one of the first residents of Stalin-Allee. It starts from Café Sibylle, Karl-Marx-Allee 72.

52__ The Kaulsdorf Church Tower
Monuments of love

It is a custom that almost nobody knows today. When the attic rooms of the church in Kaulsdorf were cleared out, oval boards with writing that could hardly be deciphered were thrown into a skip – and only just rescued in time from being taken to a rubbish tip.

They are the oldest surviving »death-crown panels« in the March of Brandenburg. These plain Baroque panels dating from 1716, which are now on display in the church tower, are evidence of a custom that was widespread in Brandenburg in the 18th and 19th centuries. When a child or a young person died, the parish put on a wedding for the deceased: marriage was considered the biggest and finest festivity in life.

If a girl died, the boys from the village plaited a funeral wreath of flowers for her, and the girls did the same when a boy died. The wreath was then placed on the ledge of the death-crown panel – as a substitute for the wedding crown that the deceased would no longer be able to have. The decorated panels were then hung up in the church. They were called »memorials of honour«, »crowns of memory« or also »monuments of love«.

Funeral weddings exist in many different cultures around the world. The idea is that the unmarried deceased person should not pass into the world of the dead without enjoying the most important event in his or her life – and above all should not take revenge on the living as a result of discontent about the celebration that never happened. Christianity adopted this heathen custom – and turned the funeral wedding into a Christian heavenly wedding.

Theodor Fontane, who walked through the March of Brandenburg in the 19th century, described the decorated panels that he saw in the churches there: »One crown next to another, embroidered ribbons; between them immortals' wreaths, colourfully mixed.« The two panels with white lettering from Kaulsdorf have been given a worthy place up in the church tower.

Address Jesuskirche Kaulsdorf, Dorfstrasse 12, 12621 Berlin-Hellersdorf | **Transport** S5, U5 to Wuhletal; bus 164, 398 to Alt-Kaulsdorf/Chemnitzer Strasse | **Opening times** Sun 11am–noon and by arrangement, tel. 030/56772333 | **Tip** A quest: before the church tower, which had been destroyed, was restored in 1999 in the Gothic style, it had a temporary roof. This roof is still in use. Where is it?

53 ___ Kleist's Tomb

And found immortality …

So this was the view that the two of them, who had decided to die, chose for their last hours on that gloomy day, the 21st of November 1811: from the rise there is a view over the choppy waters of the Kleiner Wannsee, sheltered on both sides by oak trees and fine houses. Heinrich von Kleist, »for whom there was no more help on earth«, as he wrote in a farewell letter, and his beloved, Henriette Vogel, who was terminally ill with cancer, had planned everything precisely and wished to meet death here, as Kleist's letter continued, »with inexpressible joy«.

They had taken lodgings in an inn on the opposite bank. Later the landlady related that the poet and Henriette Vogel had betrayed no sign of fear or disquiet, but had even ordered coffee to be taken across to the other bank, and had asked for it to be brought over there along with a small table.

As burial in a cemetery was not permitted for suicides in those days, they were interred at the place where Kleist shot first Henriette Vogel and then himself. The two gravestones are plain, and do not attempt to steal the show from the water, the oak trees and the climbing ivy. The original inscription was removed by the Nazis because its author, Max Ring, was a Jew: »He lived, sang and suffered / in a dark and difficult time, / he looked for death here, / and found immortality.« The new inscription is a well-known line from Kleist's play »The Prince of Homburg«: »Now, o immortality, you are all mine.«

The secluded and untouched character of this place harbours a profound intimacy – which, however, could soon come to an end. There are plans to remodel it to commemorate the bicentenary of his death in 2011 with a path, furnished with information boards and audio-points, leading from the lake shore through the beautifully neglected park – and throwing light on Kleist's life at the site around his grave.

HEINRICH VON
GEBOREN 18...
GESTORBEN 12. OK...

Address Between Bismarckstrasse no. 2 and no. 4, 14109 Berlin-Zehlendorf | Transport S 1, S 7 to Wannsee; bus 114, 118, 218, 316, 318 to Wannseebrücke | Tip Cross the lake: steamers depart in all directions from the pier on Wannsee.

54__ The Korean Garden
No entry for evil spirits

Almost everyone who comes across them has to laugh, whether they want to or not. But the two grinning faces also perform an important task with a serious purpose: they have been placed there to prevent evil spirits from coming into the village and causing trouble. »Zang Sung« is the name for the spirit posts, which look like totem poles and guard the Korean garden in »Gardens of the World« in Marzahn.

The Seoul Garden, which is situated between the Balinese Garden and the Japanese Garden, was laid out in Marzahn under the direction of a Korean garden planner and was made by Korean craftsmen, mainly using Korean materials. It is much more than a garden, however: the laughing wooden faces are guarding a whole residential ensemble, covered with dark, curving tiled roofs. The paths, gates, walls and stairs lead through a rustic courtyard. Visitors are guided through it according to a specific route – and as they pass through, they discover a whole, unexpected view of the world in all the corners of the small complex. The presence of the spirits is especially conspicuous.

Shamanism is still alive and thriving in Korea today. The shamans – almost all of whom are women – attempt to establish contacts between people and spirits.

There are various shamanic rituals, many of which are specially held for the village and its community. In the Korean garden, too, signs of these rites of evocation are present, for example in the two »Buk So« figures that protect the village and its residents from fire, floods and disease, or in the shamanic spirit masts, which look like poles with abstract birds at the top. They are intended to convey human prayers to the spirits.

But whether the threshold in the entrance gate really has the purpose of tripping up the evil spirits, as one visitor surmises, is a different matter.

Address Eisenacher Strasse 99, 12685 Berlin-Marzahn | **Transport** Bus X69 to Kienberg-strasse; bus 195 to Erholungspark Marzahn | **Opening times** April–Oct Mon–Fri from noon, Sat, Sun, public holidays from 9am to dusk | **Tip** The labyrinth: in »Gardens of the World« you can test your sense of direction in the maze.

55 Krausnickpark
An unexpected hidden corner

The houses give the impression that they are trying to keep their secret from the busy masses of people on the streets. And they do this very successfully. The spaces between them, where you would normally expect to find grey backyards with rubbish bins and bicycle racks, remain out of sight.

Only a single gate with railings leads inside, at the centre. Most people, however, rush past in a hurry. They see the synagogue and Museum Island on the left – and have no time to discover this special place.

This means that Krausnickpark remains leafy and intimate. The residents have planted gardens all around their terraces, where children can get lost on hilly grounds between the hedges and the old trees. Right at the back is the corner for hammocks. The toys are there for everyone, and picnics can be shared. You gaze on this idyll with incredulity and expect to be asked to leave again quickly. But it is a public park.

This was not always the case. On the main road leading out of the city towards Spandau, a pleasure garden was built in the 18th century – as happened in many suburbs of Berlin. It was adorned with flower beds, fountains, orangeries and pavilions. The Vierhuff'sche Garten, as it was known, was there exclusively to provide a diversion for the genteel classes. One hundred years later a society leased the land, remodelled the gardens in the park, and staged open-air plays and concerts, later balls too, for its members. The members of this society, the Therbusch'sche Ressource, belonged to the upper middle class.

By 1990 the area was in poor condition and had been divided up. Part of it was used for selling second-hand cars. Plot by plot the residents then leased the land behind their houses. They have breathed new life into the old park and opened it for everyone. The houses around help to ensure that the garden does not get overcrowded.

Address Oranienburger Strasse 19/20, 10178 Berlin-Mitte | Transport S1, S2, S25 to Oranienburger Strasse; S3, S5, S7, S75 to Hackescher Markt; tram M1, M6 to Monbijouplatz | Opening times Daily 9am–6pm | Tip Take a snack with you: Beckers Fritten at Oranienburger Strasse 43a serves home-made French fries with lots of sauce.

56_ The Last »Platte«
Tangible GDR

Living in a »Platte« – everyone knows what this abbreviation means:
»Plattenbau« is the term for residential blocks made of prefabricated concrete, and the word »Platte«, which means »slab«, once meant
much more than an ugly building. It was the epitome of modern
living. It meant running water, central heating and a creche for the
kids in a green courtyard. In the 1970s the GDR started to build
these places for modern living around the historic village centres of
the East Berlin suburbs. The members of the party youth organisa-
tion FDJ (»Free German Youth«) were called on to join in the work –
and in only ten years 42,000 flats of the type known as »WBS70«
were constructed in Hellersdorf.

Today you can take a look at modern life as it then was in the last
remaining unrefurbished 61 square metres of »Platte«. A ground-
floor flat in Hellersdorf contains all the heritage of a chapter of German construction and residential history, gathered from the neighbouring flats before the whole building was renovated.

There is lots of flowery wallpaper, wall cabinets with a colour
television and crochet-work on the coffee table. In the child's room
there is a sandman next to a Soviet CCCP plastic astronaut, and in the
drawer below it vinyl records from the Amiga label and a Magica
child's projector. Everything is in its place – and the collection is far
from complete. People still bring along things for the museum flat.

Best of all: here you are allowed to do what you otherwise cannot do in other people's homes. Visitors can open the drawers, take
packets out of the kitchen cupboards and even look in the bedside
cabinets in the bedroom. In this way you can browse through life in
the old days, bit by bit. In a drawer in the hall beneath the mirror
where coats were hung lies the so-called house book, a green note-
book with yellowing paper in which someone in the block who was
linked to the Party recorded, which tenant in the block received un-
registered visits. This too was part of life in the »Platte«.

Address Hellersdorfer Strasse 179, 12627 Berlin-Hellersdorf | **Transport** U 5 to Cottbusser Platz; bus 195, 197 to Spremberger Strasse | **Opening times** Sun 2–4pm or by appointment, tel. 0151/16114440 | **Tip** Model flat: opposite the museum flat you can see a model flat in a »Platte« refurbished by the housing association.

57___The Ledges on the Bridge
The most romantic place in Berlin

Hardly anyone in Berlin knows the name of this bridge. For most people it is simply »the pedestrian bridge«. Here Berlin presents all its old glory. Next to the water, proud and above any change in fashion, rise the Alte Nationalgalerie, the Berliner Dom (Protestant cathedral) and the old Börse (Exchange). But the thing that makes this place so outstanding – as we boldly promise in the subtitle above – is its location. When the sun goes down above the river Spree like an orange ball with this backdrop ...

Unfortunately this is why the most romantic of all Berlin's bridges gets extremely crowded – with accordion players, folding tables covered in fur hats, stones from the Wall and mamushka dolls – not to mention the countless tourists themselves, who wander across the bridge every day between the museums and the next item on their itinerary.

For this reason the pedestrian bridge ought really to lose its romantic image – were it not for two secret islands that you can escape to. If you truly want to enjoy sunset in Mitte district, you have to climb over the stone parapet. On both sides of the curved bridge is a projection with room for two or three people to sit. At a stroke you have got away from the overwhelming bustle on the bridge. You are suddenly on your own.

Sometimes a hand is waved from below from one of the river boats, which in fine weather sail round Museum Island at the rate of one a minute on their tours of the city, and sometimes a couple of heads that have managed to lean far out over the bridge will disturb the intimacy of the spot.

Otherwise the view over the water and the sublime centre of Berlin is spoiled by nothing at all. The sun warms the stones – and even the melodies played on the accordions now seem to match the picturesque scene, your outstretched legs and the evening sun shining on your face.

Address Friedrichsbrücke, 10178 Berlin-Mitte | Transport S 3, S 5, S 7, S 75, tram M 4, M 5 to Hackescher Markt; tram M 1, 12 to Am Kupfergraben | Tip Buchhandlung Walther König, Burgstrasse 27, is a well-stocked bookshop with the right reading material for sunset behind the parapet of the bridge.

58__ The Light Well

Built for Berlin's airwaves

Looking up makes you feel tiny. It's five storeys up to the glass roof, and on each floor, through the gaps in the balustrade of yellow brick, you can see the same arrangement of doors around the light well on every floor. It is visually perfect. And the layout is even more perfect. This ordered appearance leaves you in no doubt: the building was erected for a purpose. Indeed, it was never used for any other purpose than the one for which it was built: broadcasting.

In 1931 Hans Pölzig was one of the first architects to design a building that was planned exclusively for the purpose of making radio broadcasts: the Haus des Rundfunks. The great auditorium, above all, was a phenomenon in its time. The 1081 tilting seats had special perforations so that the acoustics of the room would be the same with and without an audience. In addition it had its own foundations, so that sound waves from the street could not be transmitted into the auditorium via the floor.

Only a short time after the Haus des Rundfunks opened, the agenda was less about the purity of sound than about pure propaganda. The National Socialists broadcast their Reichsfunk from here. After the war, although the Haus des Rundfunks was in the British sector, the Red Army occupied it. And after the founding of the GDR, the Soviets continued to broadcast from the British zone – which led to a dispute, of course. The British army barricaded the building.

In 1954 the Russians took the technical equipment and moved to a new radio centre, but left guards behind. Not until 1957 was Sender Freies Berlin (Free Berlin Broadcasting) able to go on air for the first time.

Today Rundfunk Berlin-Brandenburg makes radio and TV productions in the studios. The Berlin Symphony Orchestra rehearses in the main auditorium – and after all the political turmoil, the paternoster in the light well goes round and round, rattling ceaselessly.

Address Haus des Rundfunks, Masurenallee 8–14, 14057 Berlin-Charlottenburg | Transport S 41, S 42 to Messe Nord/ICC; U 2 to Theodor-Heuss-Platz; bus M 49, 104, 218, 349 to Haus des Rundfunks; bus X 49, X 34, 139 to ICC | Opening times Open at all times | Tip Studio tour: on Mondays at 6pm and Saturdays at 5pm there are free tours of the rbb studios and the historic building – bookings Mon–Fri 10am–5pm, tel. 030/9799312497.

59_Lilienthal Castle

Not fortified

Decorated posts, with chains on both sides. That can only mean one thing: the path to the front door crosses a drawbridge! And this is only one of many details that make this mansion into a little knight's castle, and give it a romantic, fairytale appearance.

Gustav Lilienthal, the brother of a famous pioneer of flight, Otto Lilienthal, built this castle in 1893, as well as a whole series of country houses with turrets, oriel windows and crenellations in the district where he lived. There was an enormous demand for Lilienthal's castles.

Today a reminder of the family of the pioneer of flight is given not only by a commemorative plaque in the front garden in Lichterfelde, but also by Anna Sabine Halle, a granddaughter of Gustav Lilienthal. At over 90 years of age she lives in the castle and preserves its heritage by passing on the history of the house and its occupants. With luck you can find Frau Halle on the bench in the rose garden in front of the house – in which case you will find out about the architectural characteristics of the building and also what lies behind the walls.

And the more you hear, the clearer it becomes that the castles are in fact the opposite of what they appear to be at first sight: they are not fortresses in which the residents seal themselves off, the towers and battlements are not meant for defence, and the drawbridge is not intended to be pulled up.

Gustav Lilienthal's houses are never pompous, and their decorations are never mere ostentation. Instead these playful motifs from times past surround a homely design that is fully adapted to the needs of the occupants.

And every decorative element has a function: the ventilation ducts have outlets in the turrets, and the drawbridge leads across the moat of the house, which in turn exists so that the cellar rooms get enough light through large windows.

Address Marthastrasse 5, 12205 Berlin-Steglitz | Transport Bus X 11 to Holbeinstrasse; bus 188 to Baseler Strasse | Tip Otto Lilienthal memorial: in 1894 Otto Lilienthal built a mound, his »Fliegeberg«, to try out gliders. Today the mound at Schütte-Lanz-Strasse 41–43 is a park and place of memorial.

60__ The Lohmühle
Independent urban life

The no-man's-land on the canal was a bare patch of ground. Even when this not-very-green strip of greenery was no longer on the border, the earth still hardly recovered. In winter it became muddy and lacked vegetation, while in summer the wasteland was a dusty piece of terrain. But it is hard to imagine this today, when you stand on the disused railway crossing and look across the Lohmühle caravan community on the canal bank.

This patch of land has still not been built on, and in a sense remains no-man's-land, but since 1991 an independent ecosystem of a kind that exists nowhere else in the city has arisen on the site around a changing group of caravans.

Between a little pond and a charming thicket stand a couch and several chairs. A small bridge leads over the pond. In the gardens around the caravans are rows of raised flower beds, a scene of luxuriant growth and blooms in an impressive mixture of the wild and the cultivated, of natural seeding and planting for a purpose. The site has its own plant-based sewage system, an educational trail – and a race track for worms.

The greatest achievement, however, is probably electricity generation: the roof of almost every caravan is covered with solar cells, and several windmills turn on the site. This self-produced power not only makes the lives of the caravan-dwellers a great deal easier. The Lohmühle is also able to provide power for its own events on site and on a big stage: every summer friends and neighbours are regularly invited to jazz concerts and film screenings, and on Sundays coffee and cake are served at the open-air bar.

The contract between the local authorities and the Lohmühle, by which the association of caravan residents was appointed administrator of the site, has been extended until 2015. On its website the Lohmühle has dressed up its motto as a Berlin slogan: »Be citizens, be caravanners, be Berlin. Free space for all!«

Address Lohmühlenstrasse 17, 12435 Berlin-Treptow | **Transport** Bus M 29 to Glogauer Strasse; bus 194 to Lohmühlenstrasse | **Opening times** See www.lohmuehle-berlin.de for the latest events | **Tip** The exhibition van: in an open caravan on the canalside path, the Lohmühle tells the story of what was once a strip of land on the Berlin Wall.

61__The Maggot Machine
Bait round the clock

From the outside you can look through the glass into the various compartments but, try as you might, it is not possible to tell whether the six drawers in the converted cigarette machine really do contain what the five large black letters above them proclaim. The price for making a purchase from the machine is one euro.

Almost everybody who stands in front of the shop for angling equipment in Wedding for the first time puts it to the test and pulls out the drawer with a good jerk.

The drawer resists at first, then gives way with a little popping sound and delivers up a round green tin. The white lid perforated with small holes indicates that some living creature is waiting inside the machine to be liberated. But can they be real maggots? Little worms? Sceptics are still not convinced.

And when they unscrew the lid and remove it carefully, what they have in their hand is still a little bit of a surprise: small, shiny, armoured bodies raise their tube-like heads into the air, before burying themselves in sawdust again with a supple turn of the body. At the sight of this creeping, crawling and wriggling you can suddenly get a strange feeling in your stomach.

And now at the very latest, as always when you have bought something by mistake, you start to wonder: Why on earth did I do that? And in this particular case, the next question is not far behind: What shall I do with the maggots? Simply throw them away? Now that I have just released them from captivity?

At the very least, this situation encourages you to think for a moment or two about your shopping habits, before the maggots are left to their fate in the nearest bushes, which is what usually happens.

By the way: Angelhaus Koss refills its maggot dispenser at weekends. And, of course, real anglers don't buy the maggots out of pure curiosity, but for a good reason.

MADEN

Address Tegeler Strasse 36–37, 13353 Berlin-Wedding | Transport S 41, S 42 to Wedding; U 9 to Amrumer Strasse; bus 142 to Kiautschoustrasse | Tip How to cook maggots: these little creatures are very nutritious, and in Africa and Asia they are served deep-fried as a snack to go with beer.

62_Majakowskiring
Where the gentlemen from Pankow lived

They stand to attention with green helmets on their heads along the small, shaded cobblestone road: old street lamps on Majakowskiring, looking like tin soldiers and instantly raising memories of days gone by. The East German political elite once resided in large, pre-war detached houses, hidden behind a wall and well guarded by real, arms-bearing soldiers. This is where Walter Ulbricht, Erich Honecker and the other members of the government of the GDR led bourgeois lives – and to make sure that this was not embarrassingly noticeable in the workers' society, they shielded their private sphere thoroughly from public view.

In the West, too, the existence of this enclave in Pankow was known – and thus the name of the district quickly became a synonym for the government in East Berlin. Konrad Adenauer liked to refer to Walter Ulbricht and his regime as »the gentlemen from Pankoff« – pronouncing the last consonant, incorrectly. And the veteran rock star Udo Lindenberg wrote a song about going to Pankow to drink a glass of cognac with Erich Honecker – in order to get permission to perform in East Berlin. »Sonderzug nach Pankow« (to the tune of »Chattanooga Choo-choo«) became a cult song in 1983, not only in the East.

In response to the song, a few months later Lindenberg was invited to the Rock for Peace festival in the Palast der Republik in East Berlin, where he presented his leather jacket to Honecker – who had previously written to him that rock music was compatible with the ideals of the GDR.

After the workers' revolt of 1953, the party cadres felt insecure in the city, and in 1960 move to a protected estate near Wandlitz. Today only a few plaques testify to the past on Majakowskiring. Modern detached houses are filling the vacant plots beneath the old trees, and Erich Honecker's old house is now home to Kulti, a place for children to play.

Address Majakowskiring, 13156 Berlin-Pankow | **Transport** Tram M 1, bus 107, 250 to Tschaikowskistrasse | **Tip** Majakowski-Gasthaus: in the beer garden at Majakowskiring 63, between the old leaders' houses, the house speciality is borscht.

63 The Maltings
Careful renewal

The monk who advertises Schultheiss beer is as relaxed as can be. Visible from afar, he greets you by raising his foaming glass from the white chimney that rises above the industrial estate on the A100 road. Most people who come here are on their way to the big furniture store or the DIY shop next to the approach road. However, since 2009 a new symbol has stood proudly above the old Berlin malt factory next to the Schultheiss monk, who has faded somewhat with the years: the flag of Switzerland.

Frank Sippel is Swiss. He bought the factory, as he bought many factories before – in order to sell it again. That would have meant the continuation of what began next door with the furniture shop and the DIY store. But when Sippel visited the Schultheiss site, he changed his mind and took charge of its conversion himself. There was a significant difference to most other redevelopment projects: he had time.

Nothing is being done in a rush on this industrial area in Tempelhof. Artists now work in the buildings around the factory yard. There is a hall for events, and above all lots of space for projects and ideas.

The »malt team« proclaim their commitment to environmental awareness: in the yard stands a waste container with a closed loop for biological recycling, and on the grass behind the factory a fish pond and a bathing lake are being created.

The main building with its four gigantic chimneys, which was used for producing malt until 1996, has remained untouched. The winding mechanisms on the shafts have become rusty, and dusty cobwebs hang from the chimneys, but the last grains of barley left over from the drying process still lie on the malting-floor grid. No decision has been taken on a new use for the factory, but whatever happens here, the plan is to combine the two main principles of the new maltings: art and sustainable use.

Address Bessemerstrasse 2–14, 12103 Berlin-Tempelhof | Transport S 41, S 42, S 45, S 46, S 47 to Südkreuz (15 minutes' walk); bus 106 to Bessemerstrasse | Opening times Viewing from outside and visits to studios daily, for tours see www.malzfabrik.de and by appointment, tel. 030/755124800 | Tip Out in the sun: on the roof terrace of the Bergstübli you have the feeling of being in a Swiss mountain hut with a view of the factory yard. Lunch Mon–Fri 12.30–2.30pm.

64___The Massage Couches

Stay in good shape

Stefan Kim thought up the idea of lying on warm jade stone. As a student in Korea he attached light bulbs to the underside of a wooden bench in order to sleep better with a warm back. As a medic he knows why the combination of stones, warmth and pressure is so good for the back. Kim worked in cancer research for many years. Now, he says, he would like to help before it is too late. The twelve massage couches in the ground-floor flat in Steglitz look as if they have come from a futuristic film. Hardly a word is spoken here, and at most at a whisper. Stefan Kim folds down the cover, spreads out the woollen blanket, and goes to greet a new customer with a glass of tea.

You want to get up again immediately, as the warm jade balls that push into you on the couch from your neck down to the small of your back and all the way again are so hard and unyielding. But once you have resisted this initial urge, your muscles and nerves become wonderfully relaxed beneath the opaque plastic cover. Just occasionally, like your neighbours lying close by, you might groan a little at the pressure on some part of your spine.

After 40 minutes of this treatment, Stefan Kim pulls the cover from the couch with a sceptical look, points out the crumpled places and explains where the problems lie in your backbone.

The massage couches are not only good for the back, but also for your mental state. Stefan Kim explains to his customers how the various elements of the Korean method of natural healing work. He does not make appointments, and you have to allow for a certain amount of waiting time, as about 120 customers come every day and pay four euros for having their backbone treated. Some come simply to relax, others because they want to conquer pain.

Stefan Kim looks after every single person with great dedication. Which is why almost everyone who comes is a regular customer.

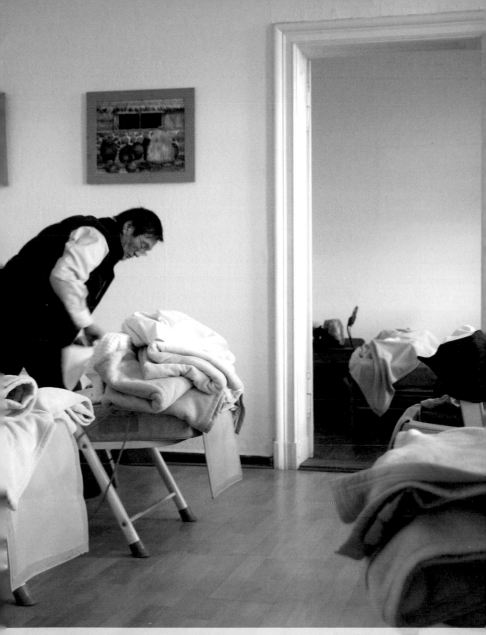

Address Dwzone Medical, Schildhornstrasse 93, 12163 Berlin-Steglitz | Transport U 9 to Schlossstrasse; bus M 48, M 85, 186, 282 to Schlossstrasse subway station | Opening times Mon – Sat 8am – 8pm, Sun 8am – 2pm, no appointments needed | Tip Art in the pool: the Art Nouveau swimming baths at Bergstrasse 90 are in use for cultural events at present. For the programme see www.stadtbad-steglitz.de

65 __ The Mediterranean House

A cathedral for ferns

In winter there is only one reason to visit the Botanical Garden: the hot-houses. From afar the enormous glass dome of the Great Tropical House shines above the snowy hills. To the right of it, looking like the castle of an ice princess, is the Mittelmeerhaus (Mediterranean House). Its decorative glass towers refract the rays of the winter sun and reflect the light in thousands of beams across the snowy gardens. The Mediterranean House is not well-known, as it is overshadowed by its more famous neighbour, the Grosses Tropenhaus (Great Tropical House).

Alfred Körner designed this building for the Royal Botanical Garden in 1910. The Great Cold House for subtropical plants, today the Mediterranean House, was built much earlier than the rest of the ensemble, and modelled on the Gothic chapel of King's College in Cambridge.

The result is impressive: a cathedral of glass with Art Nouveau decorative features and cypress trees that touch the roof inside. While this home for subtropical plants was still under construction, its rear section was already devoted to cultivating tree ferns.

That is why the oldest tropical plants in the whole Botanical Garden can be found here, beyond the spicy, stony and earthy smells that emanate from the Mediterranean section. You can read about the ferns on information panels and view their delicate fronds on the ground.

But if your eyes stray upwards along the weathered and moss-covered steel supports, all at once you notice a change of perspective: below the glass roof, huge fern fronds fan out like the leaves of palm trees. These ancient specimens of Australian trees can grow to a height of 15 metres. The air is damp and mossy, and water drips from the roof. The sun shines in through the glass. You have already taken off your coat, and all of a sudden the icy Berlin winter seems to be a far, far away.

Address Unter den Eichen 5–10, 12203 Berlin-Steglitz (a second entrance is at Königin-Luise-Strasse 106) | Transport S 1 to Botanischer Garten (10 minutes' walk); bus M 48, X 83, 101 to Botanischer Garten | Opening times Daily 9am to dusk | Tip Get married: you can tie the knot in the Mediterranean House amidst thyme, lavender and sage.

66 The Memorial in Levetzowstrasse

Unexpectedly shocking

The contrast could hardly be greater: on the spot where one of the city's principal synagogues once stood, an anonymous road passes through a bleak-looking district. No shops, hardly any pedestrians, and the only touch of colour comes from the gaudy lighting of the petrol station. That is why the monument on this corner, which serves as a reminder of the destruction of the synagogue and the deportation of hundreds of Jews from the surrounding area, had to be one thing above all: massive – and highly conspicuous.

The sculptor Peter Herbich succeeded in this task. In the middle of the pavement, which means it stands in the way, is a full-size railway truck. Rust covers every inch of its old metal. The buffers, brutal and blunt, project at the front and back. A ramp leads up to the truck. On the slope of this ramp is a marble block consisting of people who are roped together with a steel cable. If you want to go inside the truck, you have to pass these indistinctly carved people at eye-level – and then continue, creeping into the interior and bending beneath the wall of the truck, which has been cut open up to waist height. It is cramped inside. Large blocks of marble stand in the way. They too give the impression of being human: a bent torso on one side, a single hand on the other. You want to make out more but cannot see anything clearly – not only because it is too dark, and not much light enters the truck through two slits beneath the roof.

Outside at the lower end of the ramp, a steel plate rises high. Numbers have been inscribed into it: the date, the number of Jewish residents and the name of the camp to which they were taken from here. You have to bend your head back a long way if you want to grasp the extent of the horror that happened in this place alone. But it remains incomprehensible. And here, on Levetzowstrasse, that hits you unexpectedly.

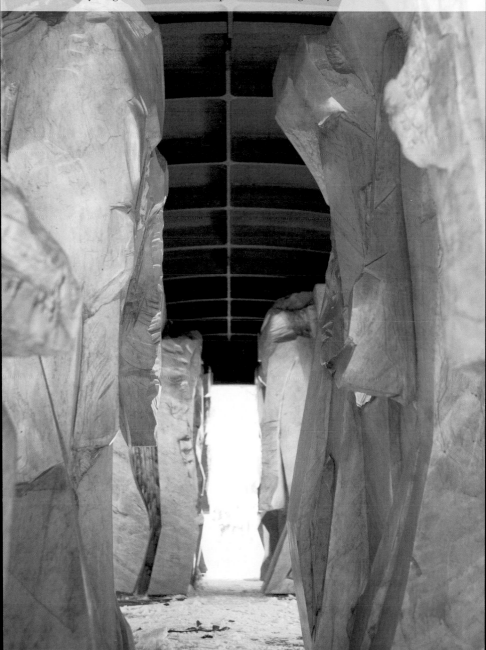

Address Levetzowstrasse 7–8/Jagowstrasse, 10555 Berlin-Tiergarten | Transport U9 to Hansaplatz (10 minutes' walk); bus 106 to Zinsendorfstrasse; bus 101, 245 to Franklinstrasse | Tip Taste and try: ProbierMahl at Dortmunder Strasse 9 is the ideal eatery for the curious. Everything is available as a small portion for tasting – so you can eat several dishes.

67 __ Meteorstrasse
On the flight path

Beyond the undergrowth on the embankment, the scene suddenly becomes infinite: a boundless evening sky, the wide expanse of the airport below it and, as far as the horizon, rows of lights that guide aircraft onto the runway. Here a road that comes directly from the heavens reaches down to earth.

First of all, far away in front of the towering clouds, two lights start to blink. They come closer, right towards you. Soon you can make out two wings, and the quiet droning becomes louder. It swells to a roar – and a moment later the huge, smooth belly of a plane has rushed over you and is ready to land. Smoke rises when the gigantic wheels touch the asphalt, and the dizzying noise of the engines echoes in your ears long after the clouds of smoke have disappeared.

Every evening a motley band gathers on the embankment: local residents with beer bottles, technology freaks with cameras and people who would like to be far away. It never gets boring here, as one plane lands after another.

This situation will not last for ever. Tegel Airport (TXL) has long been overcrowded and, like the older Tempelhof Airport, will be closed as soon as the trouble-ridden new airport is ready for service (following postponements there is still no fixed date at the time of going to press). When Berlin finally gets a big new airport suited to its cosmopolitan status, the red-and-white poles with floodlights, which are positioned all round Meteorstrasse on corners and even in front gardens, will become relics of the days of TXL and a divided city that had two airports in residential areas.

From the embankment you will then be able to watch the transformation of an enormous area that has become free, and one day stroll where the aircraft now land – and perhaps the streets around here, named after heavenly bodies, will awaken from their long semi-slumber, which by that time not even the roar of aero-engines will disturb.

Address Meteorstrasse, 13405 Berlin-Reinickendorf | Transport U 6 to Kurt-Schumacher-Platz; bus M 21, X 21, 125, 128, 221 to Kurt-Schumacher-Platz subway station | Tip The Allies in Berlin: there is a museum devoted to this theme at the far end of the airfield, at Kurt-Schumacher-Damm 42 – 44.

68__ The Mies-van-der-Rohe-Haus

Clarity, pure and simple

Simplicity makes for clarity. Among the bulky, late 19th-century houses around the Obersee lake, you can easily overlook it: the house that Ludwig Mies van der Rohe built for industrialists, a married couple named Lemke, in 1932. The L-shape of the single-storey brick building opens at the back to the lake. The windows of the two main rooms are as large as the rooms themselves, so nothing obstructs the view of the garden and sky. The building seems to be giving precedence to nature and, small and modest, to be leaving everything decorative, all colours and forms, to the plants, the sky and the water. From one of the rooms with large windows you can enter the other via the terrace. This transition makes outdoors as important for the house as indoors. It makes you ask: which was there first, and allows the other to exist at its side – the building or nature?

Around 1900 this area, today in the district of Hohenschön-hausen, which many people immediately associate with nothing but concrete tower blocks, gained importance. In the 1920s the growing settlement around Orankesee and Obersee became more and more popular, restaurants opened for trippers and the area gained its courtesy title »the Wannsee of the north«. In the 1930s industrialists and artists moved into this elegant quarter of high-class residences outside the city centre.

Today Mies van der Rohe's house is open for all visitors. The furniture that he designed for the rooms is no longer in its old place, but is displayed in Berlin's Kunstgewerbemuseum. It is planned to use the house as an art space. Artists will be invited regularly to work in the house – and to react to the special atmosphere of the rooms. The exhibitions will make it possible to explore the architecture of Mies van der Rohe from new points of view and various perspectives – and breathe new life into it again and again.

Address Oberseestrasse 60, 13053 Berlin-Hohenschönhausen | Transport Tram M5 to Oberseestrasse; tram 27 to Buschallee / Suermondtstrasse | Opening times Tue–Sun 11am–5pm | Tip Wasserturm: the brick water-tower on the opposite shore of the Obersee, almost exactly opposite the Mies-van-der-Rohe-Haus, houses a restaurant and bar. The neighbouring lake has a spot for bathing.

69_ The Modersohnbrücke
Waiting for a solar eclipse

Every evening at the same time, people come flooding from all directions and climb the slope to the bridge. Then they sit down together, in groups or couples, and all gaze expectantly in the same direction: to the west, where the railway tracks that pass under the bridge make a clear path for the rays of the setting sun.

Soon no space remains on the pipes behind the sides of the bridge, which serve as the grandstand for spectators who have come to watch the sunset. Local and inter-city trains come snaking out of the distance over the glowing orange rails, rush under the bridge with a rhythmic rattling and swishing sound, and disappear in the east, where it is already dark. Between the tracks the railway signals put on a light show. Here you can feel the city, and feel that you are part of it.

Since the bridge was rebuilt in 2002, connecting Friedrichshain with Treptow, it has become a popular rendezvous. Cyclists stop here and immerse themselves in the view of the sky. Others bring along beer and potato crisps, and sit next to each other in silent harmony as if they were at home in front of the television.

There is no need to make a date to meet on the Modersohnbrücke. As soon as you arrive, the scene on this bridge evokes a feeling of Mediterranean lightness. On balmy summer evenings, DJs make music here – there are no residents round about to complain that it is too loud.

In early summer each year there is a perceptible mood of excitement. People are waiting for something. They talk about how it was in previous years, and there is only one topic of conversation: the eclipse of the sun.

No one knows exactly when the total eclipse will take place in Friedrichshain, but one thing is sure: it happens every year, when the glowing orange ball of the setting sun disappears behind the sphere at the top of the television tower.

Address Modersohnbrücke, 10245 Berlin-Friedrichshain | Transport S3, S5, S7, S75 to Warschauer Strasse; tram M13 to Wühlischstrasse/Gärtnerstrasse | Tip RAW-Tempel: When the sun has gone down, it is worth walking over to the site of the former railway workshops at Revaler Strasse 99. There is always something going on here.

70 __ MS Lichterfelde
A boat trip for the standard fare

Berlin is opposite. The old country houses and new villas peer out with discretion and refinement between the mature trees on the shores of Wannsee lake. But here, at the harbour of Alt-Kladow, the rest of the city is an undefined mass on the other side. And you have to go a long way to get there, circling the Wannsee either to the north or the south.

The shortest way from Alt-Kladow to the city centre, however, is across the water. For the normal fare for a city trip, ferry F 10 of the BVG, the Berlin transport authority, takes the people of Kladow to connect with other routes on Berlin's transport network. Twenty minutes is the time it takes for the trip around Imchen island, past the Wannsee lido with a view of the house in which the Nazis staged their infamous Wannsee Conference, and on to the nearest railway station. At half past six in the morning, when MS Lichterfelde – the name of ferry F 10 – leaves Kladow for the first trip, she takes early commuters to work on the opposite shore.

As the day passes, the commuter ferry becomes a steamer for trippers. All the chairs are taken, the racks for bikes are full, and the ferryman has his work cut out to check all the tickets.

The first steamers on this route started operation in emergency conditions. When fuel and tyres were in short supply in Berlin in 1944, the bus service between Kladow and Spandau was suspended. From that time the ferry was used as a substitute means of transport.

By now the people of Berlin know and love their excursion on the Wannsee for the price of a normal fare, but inside the ship a notice makes it perfectly clear that the BVG ticket entitles its holder to nothing more or less than a crossing to the other side of the lake: »Keine Rundfahrt – No Sightseeing«. And the curved bar opposite the two ticket-stamping machines down in the cabin is empty and abandoned. There is only a little coffee machine in a corner on the long counter.

Address Station Kladow pier, Alt-Kladow 1, 14089 Berlin-Spandau | **Transport** F 10 ferry to Alt-Kladow; bus 134, 135, 234, 679 to Alt-Kladow | **Opening times** Crossings Mon–Fri 6.30am–7.30pm; Sat 7.30am–7.30pm; Sun 10.30am–8.30pm once every hour | **Tip** Neu-Kladow: the park of the manor house is immediately to the north of the harbour promenade.

71__The Müggelturm

»Don't be shocked, just amazed!«

In the ticket office under the stairs there is a threadbare chair. The window pane of the little cabin is broken, and a broom is lying on the floor.

You hear a dog barking in the distance and the rustling of old trees in the wind. This still-life on the Müggelberge feels like an abandoned railway station in the Wild West.

And there is a station inspector too. András Milak, who runs the snack bar in front of the tower, sells coffee, sausages and ice cream. He sweeps the ground in front of the ruined, abandoned restaurant for day trippers – and takes one euro admission from every visitor to the tower.

He speaks of a hopeless struggle – against vandalism, theft and arson. He has even printed a flyer that touchingly describes his vision, and explains the efforts he has made and his great disappointment when his snack truck was set alight in winter 2010.

»Don't be shocked, just amazed«, he calls apologetically before you walk up to the tower entrance between improvised wooden fences.

This morning he didn't manage to remove the latest graffiti from the wall of the tower, and several panes of glass remain smashed.

But as soon as you get to the top, you understand why the man who has leased the Müggelturm and watches over it, here in the middle of the woods to the south of the Müggelsee lake, has not given up: unexpectedly, the 360-degree view from this white, angular 1950s tower is overwhelming. Somewhere far in the distance, a fragile-looking little TV tower rises from the green carpet beneath low clouds, and a few cute little chimneys emit small white clouds. Far away, inconspicuous and indeed hardly visible on the horizon, is the Teufelsberg.

It is hard to imagine that a great metropolis lies between the two hills, a city full of destiny, industry and untamed dynamism.

Address Strasse zum Müggelturm 1, 12559 Berlin-Köpenick | Opening times Daily 10am–5pm | Transport Bus X69 to Rübezahl (10 minutes' walk in the woods) | Tip Berlin's summit: at 114.7 metres the Müggelberg is the highest ground in the city.

72__ The Mulackritze

Berlin's last pub from Heinrich Zille's day

It was an institution. Artists, girls from the street and people from the neighbourhood came to the »Ritze« at all times of night and day. Well-known regulars at Mulackstrasse 15 included the theatre director Gustaf Gründgens, Marlene Dietrich and the cabaret singer Claire Waldoff. And Heinrich Zille, of course, whose drawings of Berlin's low-life from the early 20th century record a tough milieu and the Berliners' incorrigible humour. Zille made many of his sketches and dialogues in the Mulackritze in the Scheunenviertel district – some of them in the upstairs room where the street girls took their clients.

Today the dark wooden bar of the pub stands in the cellar of the manor house in Mahlsdorf, a bit hidden away but completely preserved. If you stand in front of the bar in the dimly lit room, you can still feel something of the dissolute character of iniquitous Old Berlin. The impressive porcelain beer-tap looks a little neglected on the otherwise empty counter – and on the other side of the counter is the »hunger tower«, a glass case with shelves on which the landlord placed all kinds of Berlin delicacies that his customers could afford. This included meat in aspic, bread dumplings, salted eggs, gherkins and pickled herring. The old signs from the Mulackritze still hang on the wall in Mahlsdorf: »No dancing« and »Beer on tap and table service until quarter to one«.

In 1963, when the demolition of the building in Mulackstrasse was planned, Charlotte von Mahlsdorf rescued the »Ritze« – and loaded the bar shelving, the counter, the hunger tower dating from 1890 and the signs on the wall onto a handcart and took them from Mitte to Mahlsdorf.

Charlotte von Mahlsdorf was born in Berlin-Mahlsdorf under the name Lothar Berfelde. As a youth he began to collect furniture and other items from the late 19th century, and established a museum in the threatened manor house of Mahlsdorf in 1960.

ff. **Spritzkuchen**
3 Stück **25** g

Gefüllte Pfannkuchen
Stück **5** g

ff. **Ka**
3 St

Address Gutshaus Mahlsdorf, Hultschiner Damm 333, 12623 Berlin-Hellersdorf | **Transport** S 5 to Mahlsdorf (10 minutes' walk); tram 62 to Alt-Mahlsdorf | **Opening times** Wed, Sun 10am–6pm, tours by arrangement, tel. 030/5678329 or www.gruenderzeitmuseum.de | **Tip** The Orchestrion: a fine collection of music machines on the ground floor of the Gründerzeitmuseum.

73___The Multi-Storey Car Park of Neukölln-Arcaden

A bird's-eye view of life in Neukölln

Curve after curve, up you go, past intermediate storeys filled to the last space with cars. Families laden with shopping bags queue at the ticket machines. A chain blocks off the last curve to the top. If you step over this barrier for cars, you are stepping up to heaven. At the top on the asphalt, the white markings for parking spaces, with a 6 and arrows to point the direction, are already almost worn away. It is quiet. Almost unbelievably quiet. No noise from the street, not even a distant roaring finds its way to the top storey of the Neukölln-Arcaden car park. Only the monotonous drone of the ventilation emerging from inside the shopping centre through giant metal mushrooms disturbs the peace a little. You feel as if you are standing on the railing of a huge ocean liner – with the red-brown sea of Berlin's roofs stretching away to the horizon.

From up here you get a good view of life down below: in the backyard canyons you discover hidden little oases with lawns and potted plants – and in another backyard belonging to the same house, rubbish is piled up metres high. Backyards have their own rules and hierarchies. Here you see clearly how the houses are arranged in rows away from the street, with narrow gaps for backyards between them.

Something else is noticeable. Many of the tenement buildings that rose in Neukölln in the 19th century in response to a housing shortage stood empty in the 1980s, and are now coming back to life: someone is cooking in the kitchen of the flat-share opposite the car park, in a wing further away a rooftop flat is being renovated and a new wooden floor laid. The area of old housing in northern Neukölln is becoming a trendy district. It will hardly be possible for this new encounter of different ways of life to go ahead without conflicts. And the place where the conflicts will be fought out is probably the backyards.

Address Karl-Marx-Strasse 66, 12043 Berlin-Neukölln | Transport U7 to Rathaus Neukölln; bus 104, 167 to Rathaus Neukölln subway station | Tip Tours of Neukölln: historical tours, Turkish tours, tours of backyards – see this website for authentic guided tours of the neighbourhood: www.neukoelln-update.de/event/tour.

74 The Museum der Dinge

Adornment, purpose and alienation

A thing seems like an error when it is disconnected from its surroundings and loses its function. On the third floor of commercial premises in Kreuzberg, all kinds of things are suddenly left to their own devices – and the viewer looks with new eyes on items that have a strange appearance.

Design and kitsch stand idiosyncratically side by side, inventions and milestones in technology are presented – not a single inch of the showcases is wasted. A precise selection has been made, and nevertheless you can see that this cannot have been easy. Which thing out of all the thousands that surround us is worthy of presentation as a thing of its time or a thing of its material, a representative of all the things of that kind?

One cupboard stands a little away from the others. A sign on the side asks: »Foreign things?« The items behind the glass have not come far, but were collected in the area immediately around the »Museum of Things«, in shops in Kreuzberg and Neukölln: a mosque with blinking lights, a tray with tea glasses and an alarm clock with a minaret and an alarm that sounds like a muezzin calling the faithful to prayer. The other contents include a shisha pipe, a prayer chain and key rings decorated with Turkish football shirts. These are images and symbols from a Muslim culture, and for the people of Kreuzberg they long ago ceased to catch the eye. In the Turkish and Arab shops around here, they are above all popular items for tourists. A souvenir from Kreuzberg seemingly has to be as oriental as possible.

The fact that the things on show in glass cases are not merely popular ideas for a gift, but items of everyday use, is demonstrated by a perfectly normal green watering can.

In oriental countries, water vessels are placed next to the toilets for washing. And in the shops of Kreuzberg too they are sold with this purpose in mind.

Address Museum der Dinge, Oranienstrasse 25, 10999 Berlin-Kreuzberg | Transport U1, U7 to Kottbusser Tor; bus M29, 140 to Adalbertstrasse/Oranienstrasse | Opening times Mon, Fri, Sat, Sun 12 noon–7pm (with explanations: every Sun 3–5pm) | Tip Hamam: relaxation for women in a Turkish steam bath. The hamam in the chocolate factory is only one street away, at Mariannenstrasse 6.

75 Naturpark Südgelände
A victorious reconquest

Here, where nowadays only the chirping of birds disturbs the silence, the piercing screech of the brakes of a local train somewhere beyond the green undergrowth helps you imagine how once, on 60 tracks laid next to each other, countless trains braked, puffed, squeaked and hissed all together – and they must have made an unbelievable noise.

Trucks were coupled onto trains and uncoupled, locomotives were turned around, and the trains slowly trundled off in a different direction, steaming and rattling. For many years no bush or tree could survive between the tracks and the gravel on Berlin's biggest railway marshalling yard.

It has taken some 50 years – and the situation has been turned on its head. The tracks now lead through an impenetrable wilderness, a primeval forest that you cannot see through. You follow narrow paths and raised walkways across the site as if in a labyrinth, and before long you have lost your bearings. Again and again you happen upon relics from the past: the ruins of an underpass, rusty railings on a slope, gravel on the ground in the middle of woods, railway points surrounded by roots or an impressive turntable for locomotives – and the sight of these remains shows now and again that you have been walking around in circles.

In 1980, when it was planned to cut down the trees to make a new railway yard, opposition came from a citizens' initiative – and the protests were successful. The green environment was left intact, and the site with its gigantic locomotive sheds also became a place for artists.

The works of art blend into their surroundings in a way that is almost considerate – like the curving red tunnel at the place where the woods meet the grass. The quote at its entrance points the way when you take a walk across the tracks: »Art is the nearest thing to wilderness.« (Karl Ganser).

Address Prellerweg 47–49, 12157 Berlin-Schöneberg | Transport S2, S25 to Priesterweg; bus M76, X76, 170, 246 to Röblingstrasse | Opening times Daily 9am until dusk (8pm at the latest) | Tip Sunday explorations: meet at the water tower on the first Sunday in the month (from April to October) at 1pm. Open to all over five years old, free of charge.

76_ New Venice

Gardeners' heaven between the canals

Everything here overlooks the water: the garden gnomes, the chairs beneath the weeping willow and of course the couples in leisurewear in front of their garden huts. When a boat comes chugging by on the little canal, they greet it with a wave and a nod of the head. In Neu-Venedig, which means New Venice of course, every house has an entrance from the road and from the water. But the side that counts is the canal.

Visitors, too, are recommended to hire a boat from the local boat-yard and swap the road for the water: from the land, Neu-Venedig is nothing to look at.

Although you can cross the small, curving bridge on foot, all you can then do is take a longing look over the water from the middle of the bridge before you have to descend to the dusty dirt path of the little settlement.

Until the 1920s this area was no more than marshy meadowland, and the city was far away. Then, however, the meadows on the Spree were drained by means of a dense network of channels, and land gained in this way was divided up into plots – mainly for people from the city who came for watersports. No one has the right to reside permanently in Neu-Venedig. The terrain is regarded as a flood zone, which means that the gardens and houses can be flooded in case of emergency in order to protect the city of Berlin from flooding.

As this has only ever happened once, however, and that was due to a damaged lock in the post-war years, the houses in Neu-Venedig are now becoming bigger and bigger. Fine detached residences in a chic neo-Roman style with columns and painted a delicate pink are being built next to the sturdy, old-established weekend huts. This means a change in scale for the whole estate but, seen from the water, its appearance is still undisturbed, as the reeds around the landing stages and the swing chairs next to the garden pavilions at least maintain the pretence of an idyllic garden colony.

Address The area between Rialtoring and Lagunenweg, 12589 Berlin-Köpenick | Transport Bus 161 to Schönblicker Strasse or Lagunenweg | Tip Fresh fish: in Rahnsdorf near the village church, Köpenick's last full-time fisherman, Andreas Thamm, stokes up his smokery every weekend when he comes back from the lake!

77 __ The Olympic High-Dive
Scream, scream – you have to scream!

The lift is out of order. It has got stuck somewhere between three and ten metres. If you want to jump into the dark-blue water, you have to climb up the silver steps with railings on both sides, just as in every other swimming pool. Around the closed lift doors at every level, however, there still hangs an aura of great performances, of championships, world fame and medals. For this is not any old diving tower in a pool, it is an Olympic diving tower – monumental, built of stone like everything around it, situated in the shadow of the great Olympic stadium.

On the right and left, stands for spectators line the pool, but they are empty and have been closed for safety reasons. The whole complex around the stadium was built for the Olympic Games of 1936, and it exudes its own special, somewhat decayed charm. Its huge dimensions remain impressive, for example when you cross the wide spaces or take the endless path to the pool.

Twice a day the real attraction in the swimming pool, the Olympic diving tower, is opened, starting at the bottom. This is the moment when the supervisor of the pool gets up from his spot beneath a sunshade and, with all the calmness and authority of his office, removes the red-and-white chains that bar the way to the diving boards.

A gaggle of hopefuls has already assembled beneath the tower: eight would-be heroes, trembling but full of anticipation, stand at the foot of the steps. First they go up to the five-metre board, knee-length swimming trunks sticking to their legs. They all manage it. Next it's seven-and-a-half metres. Here the banter gets noisier and the group of people at the railings is larger. At the ten-metre springboard, not everyone joins in. And those who come up the steps for the second time greet the others boldly: What, are you still here? Encouragement comes from below: Scream, scream – you have to scream!

Address Olympischer Platz 1, 14053 Berlin-Charlottenburg | **Transport** S 3, S 75, U 2 to Olympiastadion; bus 104 to Altenburger Allee | **Opening times** May–Aug daily 7am–8pm | **Tip** Bell tower in the Olympic Park: it is worth going up to the viewing deck to look out over the Olympic Stadium and the city.

78__ The Open Printshop
Neukölln's new clothes

School pupils present their own slogans and motifs on the internet site. Their T-shirts bear statements such as »R for Rütli«, »Fathead« and »44 Is Ghetto«. They pose self-confidently with a challenging expression, and their hands make the sign of V for Victory to the camera.

The idea for the label Rütli-Wear was born in 2006 in the north of Neukölln. When the company SDW-Neukölln set up its workshop for screen printing there, the neighbouring streets were characterised by one thing above all: emptiness. Neukölln was an area with problems, and no-one voluntarily lived here. A cry for help from the teachers at the Rütli School resulted in even more negative publicity for the area.

The founders of the printshop wanted to do something to counteract this – and cooperated with the pupils of the Rütli School to design motifs and print them on T-shirts. In this way they created their own label. The remarkable thing about it was that the clothes are not made in China – every single item is made in Neukölln and the screen printing done by hand.

SDW-Neukölln is not only interested in motivating the pupils to design their own T-shirts and present them on the streets. Everyone can bring favourite designs or slogans to the open workshop in the form of a black-and-white copy, and print the designs themselves. After an introductory course to explain the steps in the process and the rules of the workshop, you can come again and again to print from the stencil.

It does you good to spend a day in the workshop. The sweetish smell of the ink hangs heavy in the air. While you are here, everything else around loses importance – all that matters is the print. It can truly inspire you. And in the evening, when you leave the workshop, you look at the T-shirts that come towards you on the street with completely new eyes. Which of them is a unique item?

Address Pflügerstrasse 11, 12047 Berlin-Neukölln | **Transport** U 8 to Schönleinstrasse; bus M 29, 171, 194 to Pflügerstrasse | **Opening times** Tue–Fri 10am–7pm, tel. 030 / 51059745 or www.sdw-neukoelln.de | **Tip** At the next corner you can get delicious pretzels with butter and chives at Lenaustrasse 10.

79_ The ORWO-Haus
Berlin's noisiest concrete block

Germany's first Frank-Zappa-Strasse is in Berlin-Marzahn. On the only bend in this road stands the ORWO-Haus, once the factory of the East German manufacturer of photographic film, »Original Wolfen«, abbreviated as ORWO. Musicians from all over the city fought for this building to become a place for rehearsals that they would run themselves – and they won.

There is a ghostly quiet in the long, dimly lit corridors. Old pipes run along the ceiling, and the place smells of concrete. At three o'-clock in the afternoon, almost nothing is going on in the ORWO-Haus. Only in the evening does this drab-looking prefabricated block come to life.

On seven storeys these same corridors will be filled with a dense web of sound, and a throbbing mixture of rock, metal, punk and electronic music will sound from the open windows and across the grassy plains of Marzahn's industrial zone. In this self-styled music factory, a total of 180 bands rehearse in 90 uninsulated studios.

It all began in 1998. After the fall of the Wall, the factory was empty. The red and grey building with the address »Street 13, nos. 19 –20« was administered by a property trust company. Bands moved into the upper floors on a temporary basis. For three deutschmarks per square metre they were allowed to turn the volume up to the maximum. The principle worked: those who play loudly enough themselves don't hear the others.

Things went well for a time, and the building filled up – until in 2004 the building planning authorities discovered serious deficiencies in fire protection. As no investor had been found for the premises, the tenants were given notice. After numerous protests and countless negotiations, in 2009 the ORWO-Haus association signed a contract of purchase. A further indication of this triumph over bureaucracy and planning regulations is that the ORWO-Haus now has a new address: Frank-Zappa-Strasse.

Address Frank-Zappa-Strasse 19–20, 12681 Berlin-Marzahn | Transport S 7 to Poelch-austrasse; bus M 6, 16 to Dingelstädter Strasse | Opening times For the latest events, see www.orwohaus.de | Tip Jam session: every Thursday at 9pm the ORWO musicians give a concert. Admission free! Also, don't miss the view from the roof of the block across the expanses of Marzahn.

80 The Paintbox Estate
Everything as it should be

It is a modestly sized idyll, built on a slope. Basically Gartenstadt Falkenberg is no more than one section of a street. Which makes each step on the uneven cobblestones all the more pleasurable. And probably no one walks this way once only, as no two houses are the same, and when you pass the first time it is impossible to take in at one time the countless subtle details on their façades.

The houses that Bruno Taut and Heinrich von Tessenow built for »Falkenberg Garden City« look as if they have been painted by children. They are the mirror of a world where everything is as it should be. A front door, windows with shutters, a front garden – and above all, colourful! The houses are red and black, bright blue, a tender green, chequered red and yellow. The playful, out-of-proportion arrangement of cornices and verandas, the direction in which the houses face, the mini-windows like spy holes with shutters in front – all of this was designed by the architects between 1913 and 1916 with the aim of enabling people on a low income to have a pleasant, modern style of life.

It was a sensational new idea to take workers out of rented tenements and accommodate them in leafy suburbs out on the edge of the city in small terraced houses that had gardens and were brightly painted too!

The »paintbox estate«, as it was soon called, aroused a level of public interest that is almost inconceivable today – and also met with resistance. »Ruining the landscape« and »a crime against the people's soul« were accusations that almost brought the project to a halt.

However, the mayor of Berlin, Dr Gustav Böss, issued instructions to give the architects a free hand. Thanks to him, Berliners were forced to get used to this new style of building.

Five more estates followed in the 1920s – and all of them were included on the UNESCO list of World Heritage sites in 2008.

Address Gartenstadtweg, 12524 Berlin-Treptow | **Transport** S 8, S 85 to Grünau; S 9, S 45 to Altglienicke; bus 163 to Gartenstadtweg | **Tip** The Bauhaus-Archiv: a museum at Klingelhöferstrasse 14 presents the Bauhaus, one of the leading schools of architecture, design and art of the 20th century.

81__The Pallasseum
A housing project overcomes its bad image

The building is tall, and above all long. Supported on broad walls of concrete, it covers the street and extends even further, to the grey concrete bunker on the other side of the road, finally ending on huge buttresses in Kleistpark beyond. Countless balconies with faded paint and an even larger number of TV satellite dishes make up its façade. It is 1970s public housing of the kind that you can find in every city. In the passages beneath the building you feel lost and vulnerable. The wind whistles around the concrete walls, and a plastic bag flies up a buttress.

However, on the other side of the road, an identical building presents a different picture. Lots of colourful pictures glow on the walls: a flower, a dog on a meadow, a sunset, children, a glass of tea. The photos have been stretched over the grey and white satellite dishes. The occupants themselves have chosen their own motifs – the idea was to take an image that comes to their living rooms via satellite from their far-away homelands. Almost everyone joined in this action by the artist Daniel Knipping, which was named »from inside to outside«. It is only one of several communal projects in this residential block. There is a neighbourhood café, help with homework for the kids and language courses for their parents, a residents' newspaper, evening barbecues and flea markets in summer, and of course the new name: Pallasseum.

It is not so long ago that this public housing on Pallasstrasse was known as the »social security palace«. It had a bad reputation. People avoided it. For good reasons: the doors to the building stood open, junkies' needles lay around, and people simply threw rubbish from the windows. In the late 1990s, the housing management began to make some changes in cooperation with the tenants' committee. Within a period of only ten years, they have been successful: in 1998, 100 of the 517 flats were unoccupied – but now there are waiting lists to move into the Pallasseum in Schöneberg.

Address Pallasstrasse 3, 10781 Berlin-Schöneberg | **Transport** U 2 to Bülowstrasse; U 7 to Kleistpark; bus M 48, M 85, 106, 187, 204 to Goebenstrasse | **Tip** Café Palladin: the lunch and cakes are served straight from the adjoining cookery school. Pallasstrasse 8 / 9.

82_ The Park Railway
Steaming through the Wuhlheide

Merapi is the name of a volcano on Java. And a steam locomotive in the Wuhlheide heath. For many years this little black-and-red locomotive was in service on a sugar-cane railway in Indonesia – and then it came to Berlin. Today it is standing at the main station in the park. White clouds emerge from its chimney, and its lamps shine like sparkling eyes. Wuhlheide is the place where the »Young Pioneers« of the GDR were trained as railwaymen. Today the narrow-gauge railway in the park still employs children and young people: as railway personnel.

Some 200 railway staff, the youngest of them eleven years old, take care of running the park railway at weekends and during school holidays. They sell and check the tickets, they prepare the trains for departure, and they set the points and signals. The regulations here, between the trees and meadows of the Wuhlheide, are the same as on the national rail system. Eighteen-year-olds can even become train drivers here.

The Young Pioneers' railway of the GDR was founded on 10 June 1956, railwaymen's memorial day, following the example of railways for children and pioneers in the Soviet Union, where the very first children's railway operated as long ago as 1935 in Tblisi, the capital of Georgia.

The red-peaked cap with the golden emblem of the Reichsbahn railway and the dark-blue uniforms fit well: the young railway operators' clothes were tailor-made. They are the same as Reichsbahn uniforms from the 1960s and 1970s, and are passed on down the generations, although stocks are slowly diminishing. Every now and again an ex-employee of the Reichsbahn clears out his wardrobe and brings a uniform to the park railway, as many of them still cherish their links to the little railway in the Wuhlheide. At weekends some of the very first pioneer railwaymen go out for a run with their grandchildren on the old familiar tracks.

Address An der Wuhlheide 189, 12459 Berlin-Köpenick | Transport Tram 27, 63, 67 to Freizeit- and Erholungszentrum | Opening times For the timetable, see www.parkeisen-bahn.de | Tip Sightseeing: at the park railway's Freilichtbühne station, the Modellpark presents a miniature version of Berlin.

83 ___ The Pasture Between Concrete Blocks

Win-win strategy in Marzahn

The six black Dexter cattle that graze here between tall plants and bushes are only the beginning. In Marzahn there are 1067 hectares of municipal green space, and too little money to look after it. Necessity is the mother of invention – and on wasteland next to an estate of concrete blocks, which needs to be mowed at least once a year, sturdy cattle with long, curving horns are now at pasture.

This is not just beneficial for the cattle, the communal finances and the local residents. It has other, small-scale effects. The nature protection station in Malchow has found out that keeping cattle also produces a greater variety of species. When mowing machines were regularly used to cut everything right back, only two or three kinds of plant could survive here. The cattle allow more species to grow, which in turn attracts insects and birds.

The cattle are easy to look after: they stay outdoors all year round, need no stalls and require no fodder. Marzahn has already identified 60 more meadows and patches of waste ground that could be used in this way.

The idea is not new, and there is a name for it: urban agriculture. The intention is to make unused land in the urban environment useful again. The models for this are cities in developing and threshold countries, where people plant their own fruit and vegetables and keep animals in order to support their existence.

Cows are still an unusual sight in Marzahn, but the first little herd on the river Wuhle has been a success. It sets an example for a new use of wasteland in the city. In other districts of Berlin, too, animals are being employed to look after green spaces: in Lichtenberg Pomeranian sheep are keeping down the vegetation in a cost-effective and environmentally friendly way, and in Adlershof sheep have replaced mowing machines.

Address Hohenschönhauser Strasse / Hellersdorfer Weg, 13057 Berlin-Marzahn | Transport Bus 197 to Tierheim Berlin | Tip Wuhle valley trail: a trail for walking and cycling starts on the Neue Wuhle and follows this little river until it flows into the Spree in Berlin-Köpenick.

84__The Paternoster

A lift that is part of West Berlin's history

The wooden cabins rattle ceaselessly as they pass offices where people come to acquire a passport or German citizenship. They never stop, but continue at their own speed.

People in a paternoster have always been haunted by a vague anxiety, the tingling of nerves that befalls you when the cabin leaves the top floor, rounds the man-high machinery in complete darkness, and descends on the other side. These are the feelings of the journalist Doctor Murkes in a short story by Heinrich Böll. Every morning Murkes took the paternoster to his office, and each time stayed for the extra turn through the roof space, philosophising all the while about the ups and downs of life. This is also how Charlie Chaplin felt when – something that many people at that time feared – he rode up into the darkness in a paternoster and came down again standing on his head.

Paternosters have become a rarity. Since 1972 construction of these popular »carousels for pen-pushers« has no longer been allowed in Germany. New regulations on lifts prohibited them. Because of the great danger of accidents, in the mid-1990s all such open lifts were to be taken out of operation. This was greeted not only with protests, but in Munich by the founding of a »Society for Saving the Last Rotating Passenger Lifts«, thanks to which the remaining cabins are still permitted to circulate.

The paternoster in Schöneberg City Hall has been turning for half a century: it was in motion when the Liberty Bell first rang from the city hall tower to mark the end of the blockade of West Berlin. It continued through the years when Schöneberg City Hall, the seat of West Berlin's government, was the political centre of the divided city.

And it was rotating when John F. Kennedy expressed solidarity with the besieged city from the balcony here with his famous words: »Ich bin ein Berliner.«

Address Rathaus Schöneberg, John-F.-Kennedy-Platz 1, 10825 Berlin-Schöneberg |
Transport U4, bus M46, 104 to Rathaus Schöneberg | Tip The city hall tower: 638 steps
lead up to the historic Liberty Bell. Note: it rings every day at noon.

85 Platz des 4. Juli
700 metres of Hitler's autobahn dream

They lie there like wrecked ships in the sea of a city that is continually moving and developing: buildings or squares that were planned and built, but were either never completed or simply got forgotten. Like wrecks they are pillaged, sprayed with colourful paint, and then finally they disintegrate. Sooner or later, however, some of them are rediscovered – and used for completely different purposes.

This area of asphalt, as long as four football pitches, is just such a left-over wreck. It was built for Hitler as a sample. A first beginning. The plan was that four orbital roads of eight-lane autobahn should surround his new capital, Germania.

After 1945 the US armed forces took over the Telefunken site near the autobahn, which had been designed by the Nazi architects Albert Speer and Hans Hertlein, used it as a barracks and gave a name to the large square in front of this complex. What had been a broad, unreal stretch of road now became a place on the city maps: »Platz des 4. Juli«.

From that time the Americans held parades on this remaining piece of Hitler's dream of a great cosmopolitan capital city. Then the Allies departed from reunified Berlin – and the asphalted square, surrounded by deserted barracks, a cemetery and allotment gardens, was abandoned in a new era, with the ever-moving sea of the city washing all around it.

While the centre of Berlin was reinvented from scratch, here in the south-west of the city, things remained quiet. Nevertheless, life is moving on for this square: a truck with a trailer uses it to practice making turns, skateboarders leap and come back to earth with a clacking sound, and every Sunday this stretch of autobahn is overrun by visitors to the flea market.

At the same time, the wide, empty expanses will always serve as a reminder of Hitler's megalomania – the »Platz des 4. Juli« is a protected monument.

Address Platz des 4. Juli, 14167 Berlin-Steglitz | Transport Bus 112 to Platz des 4. Juli |
Tip The Berlin Wall trail: a little further south, on the Teltowkanal, is the Wall trail, and
near to here one of its most attractive sections: the avenue of cherry trees, donated by Japan
»to express joy at the unification of Germany«.

86 — The Police Museum
Heists, frauds and tricks

To enter Berlin's underworld, you go down into the cellar. Here the Berlin police force presents its most spectacular cases. Illuminated by neon lights, they have been laid out for posterity on green felt: crime weapons, clues and instruments of detection in small suitcases and leather bags.

In the far corner at the back is an old-fashioned yellow telephone box. If you open the door, the phone rings – and Dagobert is on the line. He informs you about the exact location for handing over the money. No police! The department-store blackmailer Arno Funke, alias Dagobert, led the Berlin police a merry dance for years. He was famous above all for his technical devices: Funke constructed remote-controlled vehicles for rail tracks, mini-submarines and a false container for sand, in which the money was to be placed, above a tunnel. He was finally arrested in 1994, but made the most out of this career setback, writing a bestseller entitled »Confessions of a Department Store Blackmailer«.

Further famous Berlin criminals can be found in the cellar. For example, in a thick book you can read the handwritten original file on the case of the »Captain of Köpenick«, a cobbler who posed as an army captain, robbed Köpenick town hall and arrested the mayor. The Sass brothers from Moabit, gangsters in the 1930s, are leaning against the wall wearing black coats and black hats. They escaped the police many times, boasted publicly about their booty after break-ins, and distributed money to the needy. They were probably Berlin's most popular bank robbers.

Berlin's Polizeimuseum is crammed so full of displays, glass cases and life-size constables in uniform that there is hardly space for any new crimes.

On a large panel in the middle of the room, you can create larger than life-sized identikit pictures, using eyes, noses and various mouths. Why not practise using a few well-known faces?

Address Platz der Luftbrücke 6, 12101 Berlin-Tempelhof | Transport U 6 to Platz der Luftbrücke; bus 104, 248 to Platz der Luftbrücke | Opening times Mon–Wed 9am–3pm, Thu, Fri only groups by arrangement, tel. 030/4664994762 | Tip Painting pottery: paint cups, plates and jugs, have them fired and pick them up later: Mehringdamm 73, opening times: Mon–Fri 12 noon–9pm

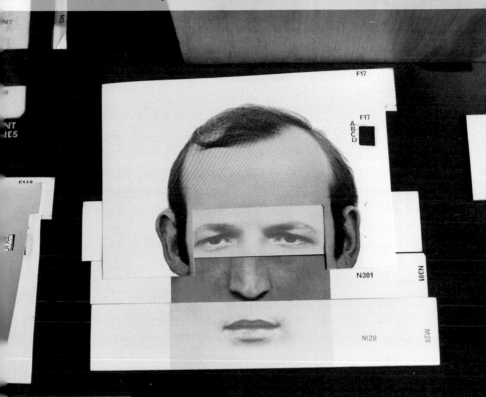

87 __ Preussenpark
Asian life in the open air

The little plastic stools are available in a big range of colours. In Europe you would normally use them as a step or footstool, but in Asia they are seats.

Generally, Asians like to sit close to the ground, as this is seen as more inviting. Asians regard the chairs used in Europe as unnatural and simply uncomfortable.

In Preussenpark the stools serve all kinds of purposes: as sales stands, as places to sit, as tables. Every weekend a whole market springs up on the grass with help of these stools, sheets and blankets, and colourful sunshades.

At first you stand a little uncertainly, surrounded by exotic, spicy aromas – but then, before you know it, the plate you are holding is laden with sweet, marinated grilled meat on a skewer, deep-fried vegetable balls, peanut sauce, sticky rice and fresh herbs. A few stools further on, fresh lime juice is being pressed. There are places to sit on the sheets behind the stalls.

This is a great place for watching the bustle and the comings and goings of Asians in the park. Every weekend – during the week too when the weather is good – Thais, Vietnamese and others come to Preussenpark. They eat together, sell their specialities and spend time with each other. There is no clear distinction between working and resting on the sheets. Right behind the lady who sells sweets – unidentifiable sugary, sticky cubes – her two daughters sit and read. Someone goes to join them, a conversation starts up, and they try some of the food. On other sheets a little further away, Thai massages are given in the shade, and a clown ties knots in balloons to amuse the children.

There is another advantage to the little stools: they are a handy size and easy to stack. As more guests, friends and relatives arrive, the circle can quickly be extended – and in the evening it takes no time to pack everything away.

Address Brandenburgische Strasse (opposite number 56), 10707 Berlin-Wilmersdorf | **Transport** U 7 to Konstanzer Strasse; bus 101 to Konstanzer Strasse subway station; bus 104 to Fehrbelliner Platz subway station | **Opening times** In good weather | **Tip** The flea market on Fehrbelliner Platz: the perfect place for a stroll after lunch, open every Saturday and Sunday.

88_ The Prinzessinnengarten
Vegetables for all at the roundabout

Cuba set a good example. When basic food supplies were in short supply there after the collapse of the Soviet Union, people in the cities joined forces to plant vegetables on their roofs, in backyards and on traffic islands. They organised self-help using seedlings and good soil, they passed on tips about cultivation, exchanged their products and swapped recipes. The two founders of the »princesses' garden« in Kreuzberg believe that urban agriculture can fulfil a need in a sustainable and neighbourly way, even in an affluent society – and they leased an area of concreted wasteland near the roundabout on Moritzplatz.

Red plastic bread baskets stacked one on top of the other act as mobile vegetable patches, and cut-open Tetrapaks are the seed boxes.

Since 2009 at the start of the growing season they have cultivated, among other plants, 20 different sorts of mint, 16 old kinds of potato plant and various forgotten strains of tomatoes.

All the plants are grown here in seed boxes. Most are harvested and used on site – in the café of the grow-your-own garden. Vegetable lasagne and salads from the mobile kitchen are extremely tasty – not only because you can see that everything on the plate has actually grown around you. On the roof above the bar you hear the humming of Kreuzberg's first bee population around a home-made wooden hive.

This attempt to establish an urban, organic, socially committed garden in the centre of the city is a success. The neighbours come along with new kinds of plants, buy the vegetables, and enjoy the fresh food in the shady little patch of woodland at the back.

The Prinzessinnengarten plans to strengthen its community approach by means of workshops. The themes will be old types of vegetables, composting with worms, bees in the city, preserving food, seasonal cooking, recycling and how to do things yourself.

Address Prinzenstrasse 35–38/Prinzessinnenstrasse 15, 10969 Berlin-Kreuzberg | Transport U8, bus M29 to Moritzplatz | Opening times In the gardening season daily 1pm–10pm | Tip A place to work: in the neighbouring Betahaus you can rent office space for a day, a week or longer. For information see www.betahaus.de.

89 _ Rabbit Island

Carefree city life

Word seems to have spread in the animal world: if you are smart, move to the city. There are no hunters there, but you find plenty to eat without having to go hunting yourself.

So their numbers are constantly increasing: foxes, wild rabbits and wild boar have settled in well in their urban habitat. They have got used to living with noise, bright headlights and the smell of people everywhere.

Five main roads meet at this crossing, and rabbits lead a pleasant, carefree life surrounded by asphalt arteries. The area in the middle is a maze of rabbit holes and passages. If you didn't hear the vibrations and roar of the subway trains beneath, you would have to worry that the whole traffic island might simply subside one day. In the mornings and evenings there are scores of wild rabbits on the scanty grass.

To call them wild, however, no longer fits the bill. They show no trace of fear whatsoever. If someone comes near, they just hop a few paces further away – not too far, just enough to keep the right distance. And then you make a discovery: food has been laid out in front of the entrances to their holes. You find a heap of peeled carrots, another pile of dried rabbit food – and a little further away: rabbit litter!

It's no wonder the animals have ceased to be shy of humans. Of course it is possible that one of Berlin's foxes might approach the island, but this is not very likely. Foxes too have changed their habits since leaving the woods. It has been observed, for example, that at night they go either to school yards and take the kids' lunch packets out of the waste bins, or – and this is a very popular destination for foxes – they head for old people's homes, where they wait under the windows for the evening meal that senior citizens often prefer to give to the animals – without knowing it – than to return plates with the meal half-eaten.

Address Bundesallee/Hohenzollerndamm, 10779 Berlin-Wilmersdorf | **Transport** U 3, U 9 to Spichernstrasse; bus 204 to Spichernstrasse subway station | **Tip** No feeding! Putting out animal food is not allowed, and is punishable with a fine of up to 5000 euros.

90__ The Refugee Camp in Marienfelde

The first stage in a new life

For the mother who fled to the West, for example, and was then faced with a payment of 50,000 marks to someone who would arrange for her husband and children to follow. Or for little Regina, who was told to put on three dresses one on top of the other on a hot day for an excursion that was nothing of the sort – and then refused to pull on thick jogging pants as well. Countless people fled from the GDR alone or with their families. Whatever their reasons for taking this irrevocable step, and whichever corner of the GDR they came from – for all of them, the first stop in the West was the camp in Berlin-Marienfelde, which the city authorities set up in 1953. By the time the Wall fell, around 1.35 million people had moved on to a new life from here.

Today a place of memorial in the building shows what these first steps in a new life were like. New arrivals first had to attend to the process for emergency admission to the country. Each was given a list of procedures and had to undergo checks in twelve different stages, until permission for admission to the camp was granted.

The museum has now recreated this bureaucratic obstacle course. An original procedure list hangs on the wall. Next to it a machine dispenses numbered queuing tickets, and beyond are twelve identical doors: when you open them, questions about your escape are asked, medical certification is issued and the authorities of all three Western allies have to exclude the possibility that you are a spy, before you walk up the stairs to the upper floor. Those who came to a room with bunk beds one above the other here were usually allowed to move on after about two weeks – and their new life began. Today people all over the world are still fleeing from repression in their home countries. And since autumn 2010 Marienfelde has been an emergency camp for refugees once again. This time for asylum seekers.

Address Marienfelder Allee 66, 12277 Berlin-Tempelhof | Transport S 2 to Marienfelde;
bus M 77 to Stegerwaldstrasse | Opening times Tue–Sun 10am–6pm | Tip The place of
memorial arranges and acts as moderator for discussions with former refugees and organises
a guided tour for children one Sunday in the month.

91 Reichenberger Strasse

Everyday archaeology

Every street has its own face. It takes its character from the shops, from the way the sunlight falls at different times of day, from its own special smells.

Small children learn to understand the world in the street where they grow up. They make their way to the bakery, they have to pass dark doorways, they watch the people standing at the bus stop, and they feel afraid of the dog from the house next door. Everyone gets to know his or her own street in this way. In a sensual way. Often you don't notice this until you come back one day to a street where you previously lived for many years.

There is an alternative way to get to know a street: to search for its history and to understand how it has changed. In Reichenberger Strasse the traces of the past have a fixed shape. On the corner of Manteuffelstrasse rails run along the middle of the pavement, and between them horseshoes have been set into the uneven cobblestones. The horse-drawn tram once went along here.

At irregular intervals you come across square concrete slabs on the broad pavement. They are not particularly conspicuous, and about as large as manhole covers. Tools have been embedded into the concrete: spanners, pliers, a cog wheel – and at the corner of Ohlauer Strasse you can even find a piano keyboard that has been turned to stone. The piano maker Bechstein once had an outlet on this spot.

The history of the city has been written – and the old story is continually being overwritten. There are many ways of writing it, and all of them show the life of a neighbourhood and a street from a different angle.

Most are of short duration, like graffiti or artists' actions. The mosaics cast in concrete last longer. They are not big eye-catchers, and even the shop owners today no longer know what they mean – but they allow the street to tell its story.

Address Reichenberger Strasse, between Manteuffel- and Lausitzer Strasse, 10999 Berlin-Kreuzberg | Transport U1 to Görlitzer Bahnhof; bus M29 to Ohlauer Strasse | Tip Parsley and fresh mint: one block away on the other side of the canal, a market is held on Maybachufer every Tuesday and Friday.

92 The Regina Martyrum Memorial Church

Overcoming feelings of anxiety

Enormously high, dark walls enclose a completely empty square. From the other side all that can be seen are the rustling tips of poplars, which have now grown so high that they look over the wall. In front of you lies a paved square, and behind you the gigantic, angular bell tower rises in a corner between the walls. You can't help feeling threatened and vulnerable. Your instincts take over with such force that rational thought is powerless against them.

The stark massiveness of this place is deliberate. The dark square in front of the memorial church of Maria Regina Martyrum was designed to look like a yard where prisoners assemble – in memory of victims of the Nazis who were murdered nearby in the prison and place of execution at Plötzensee. Just as the space in front of the church demonstrates darkness and menace and makes them perceptible, the bright rectangular memorial church on the square is a symbol of hope. Built in 1963 by Hans Schädel, the architect in charge of the cathedral in Würzburg, the memorial church with its façade of white pebbles seems to hover on the concrete pillars that support it. Inside, a stairway with 33 steps leads up to the church. Light shines into the high space only through narrow openings on either side of the big altar painting and beneath the ceiling. The effect is impressive: it seems as if there were no solid roof over the space, as if the tons of naked concrete had been raised aloft and were floating there.

Sisters of the Carmelite Order, who live a life of silence and prayer in the convent next to the church, take care of this place. The Carmelites preserve the memory of the victims of Plötzensee and pray for peace in the chapel daily at midday. It is good to know that in the unimaginably large city of Berlin, prayers for peace are said every day at the same time.

Address Heckerdamm 230, 13627 Berlin-Charlottenburg | Transport U 7 to Jakob-Kaiser-Platz; bus M 21, 109, 123 to Jakob-Kaiser-Platz subway station | Opening times On request and for church services. Information: www.karmel-berlin.de, tel. 030/3641170 for guided tours for groups | Tip Candles: the convent shop sells products from its own production – for all occasions, not only religious events …

93___The Ring on Potsdamer Brücke

Art as an exclamation mark

There are many of them: places in the city that are not really places at all. No one is aware of them. They have no significance or even purpose. And here is one of them: a yellow-painted railing with no particular design on a bridge that crosses the Landwehrkanal. A bridge that, to make matters worse, is also a traffic island, which increases the tendency to hurry past. The only thing in mind here is to get to the next traffic light quickly.

You can cross Potsdamer Brücke like this many times before something makes you pause: the ring on the railing has always been there. It is not a life-saving ring. So what is it? And how did it get on the railing? After a closer look at this object, you come – well, to no conclusion at all! It is a closed ring made of bronze – and no trace of anything on the ring or the railing explains how it was attached to the metal supports.

Norbert Radermacher is the name of the artist whose intention in making the ring on the bridge was exactly this. His works are meant to make you stop and think. They are out to catch an unexpected glance by someone hastening past – and cause a surprise. On the other side of the bridge is the Neue Nationalgalerie, where people who cross the bridge in a hurry have perhaps reached their destination, in order to look at art in a proper, prepared way.

For the exhibition »1945–1985, Art in the Federal Republic of Germany« Rademacher welded the ring on the bridge railing without official permission. It was listed in the exhibition catalogue, but the illustration only showed part of the railing, without the ring. There is no sign on the bridge to explain that this place is part of an exhibition. Even people who want to see it have to discover it by chance. In 1993 the work was simply removed when the railings were painted yellow – since when a copy has been attached to them.

Address Potsdamer Brücke across the Landwehrkanal, 10785 Berlin-Tiergarten | Transport U 2 to Mendelssohn-Bartholdy-Platz; bus M 29, M 48, M 85 to Potsdamer Brücke | Tip Lunch-time concerts: every Tuesday at 1pm the Berlin Philharmonic play chamber music for half an hour in the foyer of the Philharmonie, Herbert-von-Karajan-Strasse 1. Free admission!

94_ The Sehitlik Mosque
Open for encounters

As a guest you try to do things right. On arrival you are informed in a friendly but firm manner that you are only allowed to enter the mosque in stockinged feet. Shoes have to be taken off at the top of the outdoor marble steps and put in the allotted space inside next to the door.

But when the ground is cold and wet, it is not so easy to untie your second shoe with your foot in the air without losing balance and blocking the entrance. While you are performing this unaccustomed balancing act, members of the congregation come up the steps, slip nimbly out of their shoes without even looking, while switching off their mobile phones at the same time, and pass you, entering the mosque to pray.

In the bright interior with all its stained-glass windows and colourful ornamentation, the dominant tone is the warm turquoise of the carpet that covers the whole floor of the mosque. Whispering, you remain standing at the entrance.

However, the rule about shoes seems to be the strictest regulation in this place of worship, as guests immediately receive a friendly greeting. The mosque is always pleased to have visitors. It is also an open house, which means that everyone is permitted to talk aloud here and to look round everywhere.

Members of the congregation are pleased to answer questions about the mosque and the Turkish cemetery in front of it. There is of course no objection to taking photos – but not of the people praying, please, as then you would only see their backsides, as the official explanation points out. The Sehitlik Mosque is open for all – and this is the atmosphere that it conveys.

A sign hangs on the steps that lead up to the tower: »Do not be alarmed if loud singing begins« – this warning should certainly be taken seriously, as here the muezzin utters his call to prayers via loud-speaker.

Address Columbiadamm 128, 10965 Berlin-Neukölln | **Transport** Bus 104 to Friedhöfe Columbiadamm | **Opening times** Daily from first to last prayers – for times of prayers and tours, see www.sehitlik-camii.de or tel. 030/6921118 | **Tip** Werkstatt der Kulturen: in addition to the annual Karneval der Kulturen, the »workshop of cultures« at Wissmann-strasse 32 organises many other cross-cultural events.

95 _ Siemensstadt Station
Traces of time

All that remains of the station clock is a rusted, empty ring. It hangs hollow and ghostly from the roof. The hands that once counted the minutes until the start of the shift at Siemensstadt station are missing, and so is the clock face. Sounds that could once be heard echo in the quiet of the deserted platform: squealing brakes, the slamming of carriage doors, many feet hurrying to the steps, the factory siren wailing for the start of the shift. The Siemens trains released thousands of workers from all over Berlin at the gates of the factory. At peak times trains with up to twelve carriages stopped here every two minutes.

When you stand on the platform and look across at the huge brick buildings of the Siemens factory, the dominant feature is the big clock tower in colossal 1930s style. It leaves no doubt about the fact that measured time rules here. Speed was of the essence when the cable factory, the first of the plants here on Nonnendamm, was built around 1900. A rough, rectangular block, it rose amidst fields and meadows. Then the railway connection came. Within a few decades this was the site of an industrial complex such as the world had not yet seen. Tens of thousands of workers, engineers and office staff ensured that cables and transmitters, radios and washing machines, locomotives and steam turbines were exported all over the world from here. In 1930 the surrounding Nonnenwiesen area became a residential district for the workers, a big settlement named Siemensstadt.

For the last 30 years no more trains have run on these tracks with their four stations, and a company called Siemens Technopark is looking for tenants for the unused offices in the monumental brick building.

On the neglected platform only the growth of birch trees and dense brambles records the passing of time. This is no longer a place for arriving at. But a place to stop for a moment.

Address Rohrdamm, at number 83, 13629 Berlin-Spandau | Transport U7 to Rohrdamm; bus 123 to Rohrdamm subway station | Tip Siemensstadt: Karl H.P. Bienek leads tours through the industrial landscape, residential areas and up the Siemens tower. Information: e-mail khp.bienek@web.de or tel: 030/3817507.

96__ The South-West Cemetery
Burial ground for celebrities

The small, pale-grey gravestone is hardly visible any more beneath the shoulder-high box trees with dark green leaves that are stretching out their branches on all sides. These typical cemetery plants, which were once neatly grouped as spherical shrubs around the grave, have overcome every attempt to tame them and shape them in recent decades. Going further into the dense undergrowth you find gravestones that have half subsided into the ground, others that have fallen from their bases, and in front of a massive rhododendron you find a leaning, moss-covered stone bench. A few paces away stands a pompously decorated neoclassical mausoleum. In front of it, wild boar have been rummaging in the soil for food. At the Südwestkirchhof you see countless impressions of this kind, representing the interplay of life and death beneath a dense canopy of leaves.

The cemetery was laid out in 1909 outside Berlin as a municipal cemetery, because the churchyards in the city centre were full. It quickly became Berlin's most important burial place. The list of those who lie here is like a Who's Who of well-known Berliners: the painters Heinrich Zille and Lovis Corinth, the architect Walter Gropius, the publisher Gustav Langenscheidt and the industrialist Werner von Siemens.

Thanks to a newly built rail connection, the wooded cemetery with its wide avenues lined by rhododendrons became a veritable destination for trippers, and a café by the gates provided refreshments for citizens who came here on the cemetery railway from Wannsee.

After the construction of the Wall, the cemetery was in the middle of the border zone. No one was allowed to visit it without special permission. The tombs and vaults decayed, nature took over. Today you can explore the cemetery again, either on foot or in summer by hiring a bike from the cemetery's own hire station.

Address Bahnhofstrasse 2, 14532 Stahnsdorf, near Berlin | Transport Bus X1, 601, 602, 623 to Bahnhofstrasse | Opening times April–Sept daily 7am–8pm, Oct–March daily 8am–5pm | Tip The cemetery chapel: built entirely from wood in 1911. With its simple paintings and Art Nouveau windows, it is modelled on a Norwegian stave church.

97_The Spinner-Brücke

The Alpine hut at the AVUS meet

The website does not tell you where the nearest railway station is, but it gives the GPS coordinates: 52 26 min. 00 sec. north, 13 11 min. 25 sec. east. Because those who come to the AVUS meet have their own vehicles, with two wheels.

Chrome sparkles in the sun, here and there an engine roars at full power, and the owners stroll up and down at their leisure between the parked motorbikes. The Spinner-Brücke has always been their rendezvous. There used to be a small snack bar here, at the place where West Berlin's bikers met in good weather to discuss the tours they would make in the next season – or to speed along the AVUS urban motorway together. They are no longer allowed to drive fast down the AVUS, and the snack bar has turned into a restaurant with rustic furnishings and a large outdoor terrace. Diners wearing thick leather gear carry their trays somewhat stiffly to the tables. The mood here is good-humoured, and reminiscent of the atmosphere in a ski hut. This is no coincidence: the owner of the Spinner-Brücke restaurant is a passionate biker – and an Austrian.

There are two explanations of how the bridge known as the Spinner-Brücke got its nickname – which means the »crazies' bridge«. Some say that the name was obviously invented by people who don't ride motorbikes, who shake their heads at the crowd of noisy speedsters in their leather jackets with dangling fringes. Others say that the name of the bridge is much older than this and dates from the time when the first car races were held on the AVUS, and people who were mad about the technology used to stand on the bridge for hours at a time, staring at the grey asphalt and waiting to see the miracle machines that they so admired.

The start of the season on 1 May is the highlight of the year on the Spinner-Brücke – and the meet has long ceased to be a secret. Some 30,000 motorbike fans then come to a big bikers' party at the bridge.

Address Spanische Allee 180, 14129 Berlin-Zehlendorf | Transport S 1, S 7 to Nikolassee; bus 112 to Nikolassee rail station; bus 218 to Badeweg | Tip Pack your swimming things. Go a little further into the Grunewald forest and you reach the Wannsee bathing beach.

98___The Spreepark
The dream of Berlin's fairground king

Looking indestructible, the giant wheel towers over the old trees in the woods. Not everything has stood up so well to the test of time: the tracks of the miniature railway have almost disappeared in the undergrowth, and at the back a toppled tyrannosaurus rex helplessly stretches its legs into the air: VEB Kulturpark (»the people's own culture park«), fondly known as the »Kulti«, was once the biggest fun park in the GDR, a showcase place of entertainment.

The overgrown cabins of the rides are silent witnesses to a dream that collapsed. After the fall of the Wall, the fairground operator Norbert Witte had a vision for this place in Treptow: to attract visitors from all over Germany to the largest and most modern fun park in the whole republic.

With his wife he founded a company named Spreepark GmbH and invested borrowed money to make the dream come true. All that was lacking was visitors.

After the 2001 season, Spreepark went into liquidation. Shortly after that, under cover of darkness, Norbert Witte left for Peru, taking six rides from the Spreepark with him. »Fairground king on the run!«, announced Berlin's newspapers the next day. He is said to have owed 15 million euros to the state of Berlin.

In Peru things did not go well for Witte. When 181 kilos of cocaine were found in the hollow steel mast of the »Flying Carpet« in a shipping container, Witte's son Marcel was arrested. Norbert Witte went on trial in Berlin. In 2008 he was released from prison early – and since then has been living in a caravan in the middle of his broken dreams. For over ten years now, nature has been reclaiming the site all around him. In this period many people have shown interest in the Spreepark, but one after another they have backed out. The investors for a planned history park named Lost Worlds also pulled out – although this would have been a fitting name for the place.

Address Kiehnwerderallee 1–3, 12437 Berlin-Treptow | Transport S 8, S 9, S 85 to Plän-terwald; bus 265 to Neue Krugallee/Dammweg | Opening times Tours Sunday 1pm | Tip Insel der Jugend (Youth Island): an island in the Spree accessible via a bridge. Open-air cinema, concerts and a café in summer.

99__The Spreetunnel
Below the surface

Google Earth sees everything. Almost everything. But there are still some nooks and crannies that the Google camera has not yet captured. The Spreetunnel, for example, perhaps because it is so easily overlooked.

Where the Spree flows out of Müggelsee, here a small river, and continues towards the historic part of Köpenick, everything faces the water: the benches beneath huge old trees, the people on the river bank and the spacious riverside terraces of the fine houses beside the lake. Right at the edge of the little waterside promenade, inconspicuous beneath a dense canopy of leaves and hardly recognisable on the Google image, a tiled roof is supported by plain white wooden columns. Below it, steps lead steeply downwards – and descend beneath the water. »Constructed in 1926« says the sign above the steps. Since then the green-tiled Spreetunnel has connected Friedrichshagen with the heath called Kämmereiheide on the west bank of the Müggelsee.

Construction of a tunnel on the Müggelsee was a sensation. At that time ways were being sought to manage the crowds of Berliners who came here, especially at weekends. Until then a steam ferry had taken trippers across the river Spree towards the Müggelschlösschen lodge and the Müggelturm tower.

However, waiting times were long, and the ferry, in continuous operation on Sundays, was an obstacle to shipping. As the shipping authorities were unwilling to permit a bridge here, after years of debate the decision was taken to build a tunnel beneath the Spree. It was the first time in Germany that a tunnel of reinforced concrete had been placed in water. The concrete tube was laid in position by means of pneumatic pressure. And this is the reason why the old ferry pier is a quiet place today, where you can lose yourself in thought while looking out over the water – and a secret tunnel leads to the other side.

Address Josef-Nawrocki-Strasse (behind number 16), 12587 Berlin-Köpenick | Transport Tram 60, 61 to Müggelseedamm/Bölschestrasse | Tip Cross the tunnel: on a raft, for example, hired from the company »Floss und los« in Friedrichshagen, Müggelseedamm 216.

100 The Stasi Museum
Power behind a desk

There are four telephones on the desk. They look sparkling clean, although they are sullied by an infinite amount of injustice. From this desk Erich Mielke commanded the Ministry of State Security, the Stasi, for a period of 28 years. This was the state apparatus that held the power structures of the GDR together. Its means of operation are well known: pressure, fear and blackmail.

Using one of the two black telephones on his desk, Mielke could speak directly to the communications network of the Soviet bloc secret services, which was secured against eavesdropping. The third telephone, the white special phone, was the one that the leader Erich Honecker regularly used to get in touch with his secret service. The presence of power at the highest political level was reflected in day-to-day operations here in Normannenstrasse. In a large file, the museum presents original documents from this office in the Stasi headquarters.

It includes the instructions for breakfast that hung in the small kitchen next to Mielke's office, not only listing what he was to be given each morning – two eggs, bread, mustard, salt and a glass of milk – but showing by means of a sketch how breakfast should be arranged on the tray. This had to be adhered to exactly. Erich Mielke was famous for his fits of rage, which could allegedly be heard even from behind two padded doors.

By the end of the GDR, a total of 15,000 Stasi employees worked in a hermetically sealed-off area of eight hectares. The number of so-called unofficial workers has been estimated at 110,000. On 15 January 1990 the people invaded this closed-off courtyard in Normannenstrasse. Their aim was to put an end to the destruction of files, and to sort, view and make available to the public the mountains of documents kept there. The storming of the Ministry of State Security made clear the full extent of surveillance and restrictions on individuals in GDR.

Address Ruschestrasse 103, Haus 1, 10365 Berlin-Lichtenberg | Opening times Mon–Fri 11am–6pm, Sat, Sun 2–6pm | Transport U 5 to Magdalenenstrasse; train to Frankfurter Allee (10 minutes' walk); bus 240 to Schottstrasse; bus M 13 to Rathaus Lichtenberg | Tip Gedenkstätte Hohenschönhausen: a place of memorial where the Stasi detained political prisoners, and tortured many of them, at Genslerstr. 66.

101 St Michael's Church

Carrying on as a ruin

Around the Luisenstädtischer Kanal the most prominent landscape gardener in Berlin in the 19th century, Peter Joseph Lenné, drew up plans in 1843 for a district to combine living and working in the fast-growing metropolis. For the design of the square on the north side of the new district, Luisenstadt, King Friedrich Wilhelm IV expressed a wish: he wanted a church like San Salvatore in Venice to be built by the water. Within ten years a hall church with aisles and a tall dome on a drum was constructed next to the canal basin.

When you stand in front of the entrance to the church today, the impression of being in Venice hardly seems to have been impaired – apart from the absence of gondola traffic. However, if you move away just a few yards and change the angle of view, you realise that the nave of the church has been completely destroyed. The big bronze dome is standing all alone.

After it was ruined in the Second World War, the people of Berlin had a solution for the church. They placed pews in the spacious chancel, walled up the open side, and the restoration work was complete. Since then, church services have been held beneath the dome. And they still are today.

When Germany was divided into two states, the same thing happened to the congregation of St Michael's Church: the death strip parallel to the Berlin Wall passed just in front of the church square. However, the life of the congregation in the ruins did not come to an end.

In the 1980s the church authorities built a parish house in the open nave – a two-storey building with a tiled roof and window boxes for flowers that nestles at the foot of the wonderful dome. From outside not even its gable is visible. Ivy and vines grow up the remaining walls on either side of the bell tower, and the whole sight makes it absolutely clear that nothing lasts for ever. A useful lesson, not only in a church.

Address Michaelkirchplatz, 10179 Berlin-Mitte | Transport U 8 to Heinrich-Heine-Strasse; bus 147 to Heinrich-Heine-Platz; bus 265 to Michaelkirchstrasse | Tip The Engelbecken: a newly laid-out garden in the former Luisenstädtischer Kanal, later the border strip, leads from Oranienplatz to the Spree.

102__The Swings in the Mauerpark

Life at its fullest

Everyone knows that a swing makes your head clear. It calms the soul. Swinging to and fro produces a tingling in your stomach. There are far too few swings in the city. Playground swings serve their purpose for children, but no one spares a thought for the grown-ups. However, in the Mauerpark, the park on the site of the Berlin Wall, five swings with impressively long chains stand on the slope. They swing so high that your feet seem to touch the roofs on the other side of the park. You can go higher and higher, up to the sky. You can swing yourself towards the morning sun, or into the sunset.

Below, the park runs through the middle of the city, cutting a green swathe. This was once the course of the Berlin Wall. The East was at the top, the West at the bottom. The slope here meant that the border soldiers had to patrol for years on ground that fell away steeply – until in the 1980s a land swap was made, and East Berlin was able to push the border down into the plain. You can still find a few relics of this period: a surviving stretch of the second, rear wall behind the swings, colourfully sprayed, and on the main path there are walled-up holes at places where the floodlights stood to illuminate the death strip brightly and mercilessly.

Today the present at its most vivid and noisy has taken possession of these traces of the past. The Mauerpark is Berlin's liveliest stage. For flea markets, music, dance, graffiti or fashion – few places in the city are so bursting with life. The highlight, every Sunday, is the big open-air karaoke in the amphitheatre. People sit crowded together on the stone seats and join in when others sing their favourite songs.

There is no better spot in the city to take off into weightlessness and to swing to and fro between here and there. You just have to love the city when you are here!

Address Schwedter Strasse, 10437 Berlin-Prenzlauer Berg | Transport U2 to Bernauer Strasse; U8 to Eberswalder Strasse; tram M10 to Friedrich-Ludwig-Jahn-Sportpark; bus 247 to Wolliner Strasse | Tip The Chapel of Reconciliation: The Church of Reconciliation stood on the death strip and was blown up in 1985 to reinforce the GDR border defences. Today a wooden chapel stands on the site at the memorial for the Wall: Gedenkstätte Berliner Mauer, Bernauer Strasse 111/119.

103_ The Tajik Tea Parlour
A fairy tale in the city

No one discovers this hidden gem by accident. You have to know the way: first you walk up a curving staircase, take the entrance on the right-hand side to the first floor, then go left down the corridor, pass the marble hall of the palais, go through an intermediate door into the wing at the side – and in front of you there is a plain white sign: 1st floor, room 117, Tajik Tea Parlour.

Within, a world straight from the Arabian Nights awaits you: in subdued lighting, embroidered cushions sparkle on gaily patterned carpets in all imaginable shades of red and purple, while columns of carved sandalwood in the middle of the room and the wood-panelled ceiling frame a scene of oriental relaxation. A huge samovar bubbles and steams in the corner.

The »Tadschikische Teestube« was put on display at the Leipzig trade fair in 1974 in the pavilion of the Central Asian republics of Uzbekistan, Kazakhstan and Tajikistan. Afterwards these countries presented their tea parlour to the Society of German-Soviet Friendship in Berlin – and cleared out one room in a wing of their representation, the Palais am Festungsgraben, in order to make space for the gift. Since then, surrounded by Prussian splendour, room 117 on the first floor has been home to an authentic piece of the orient in Berlin.

When you take a seat at one of the low tables, you have to make a decision. There is Russian smoked tea, caravan tea and »Pushkin« tea, a black tea that is served with spices, jam and vodka. Or you order a round of tea from the samovar. But whichever kind of tea you choose, they all have one thing in common: when you order, you need to have plenty of time. In the orient the men meet in tea parlours to exchange views, to have discussions, to negotiate – or for a chat, it is said.

When you think about it, places like that have become a rarity in our civilisation.

Address Palais am Festungsgraben, Am Festungsgraben 1, 10117 Berlin-Mitte | Transport S 1, S 2, S 25, U 6 to Friedrichstrasse; tram M 1, 12 to Am Kupfergraben; bus TXL, 100, 200 to Staatsoper | Opening times Mon−Fri 5pm−midnight, Sat, Sun 3pm−midnight | Tip Two Berlin bears: in the Köllnischer Park by the Märkisches Museum two bears, Schnute and Maxi, live in a compound.

104__ The Tartan Track
»Can't keep running away«

The rush hour starts punctually. From six o'clock the six lanes in the Friedrich-Ludwig-Jahn-Sportpark start to fill up. More and more people wearing fashionably casual sports clothing converge on the gate, walk onto the dark-red oval space – and start to run, all of them in their own rhythm, in their own way.

The 400 metres of track don't get boring, because there is something to look at: people panting for breath, athletic people, beautiful people, slow people, ambitious people and people who are funny to watch.

What is going on here is not exclusively about sports and training. There is a reason why the tartan track takes first position in the top ten of places for singles in Berlin, according to one of the city's internet portals.

It is easy to see why. Here people pass each other on every circuit and can keep an eye on each other all the time while they are running, and they can also meet – if they want to – at the same time on the following day. Perhaps this is the meaning of the words that have been sprayed in English on the wall at the edge of the track: »Can't keep running away!«

Of course everyone likes to show off what he or she does best. Every evening at the edge of the stadium, a diverse open-air display of physical activity can be admired: skipping with a rope, sprinting, press-ups, kick boxing, shadow boxing – and all varieties of stretching. While doing stretching exercises you can cast your eye without restriction over the people running round the track. And those who prefer can use the stadium goal posts free of charge.

Some information for non-singles: summer mornings are a good time for running around the tartan track. Its lanes are empty, and grass sprinklers rotate on the football pitch in the middle. This helps you cool off while the morning sun shines over the rooftops – and round you the city slowly wakes up.

Address Cantianstrasse 24, 10437 Berlin-Prenzlauer Berg | Transport U2 to Eberswalder Strasse; tram M1 to Milastrasse | Opening times Daily during daylight hours | Tip The Prater: Berlin's oldest beer garden lies beneath chestnut trees at Kastanienallee 7–9.

105__ Tempelhof Airfield
An open-source project

There is nothing to hold your gaze – not even the other end of the airfield is in sight. Empty, wide and, to be honest, rather grim-looking, this big expanse of land stretches out behind the huge airport buildings. Only two broad strips of asphalt, the old runways, cut across the grass. A big space like this in the middle of the city is too much to handle when you first see it.

But anyone who thinks that a wide-open space of this kind could become boring in the long run and that it is in danger of turning into wasteland – and there is enough wasteland in the city already – is mistaken. On the contrary, since the former airport site was made available for use, something has happened that could best be compared with the idea of an open source on the internet: everyone takes advantage of the space and the opportunities it provides, helps to shape and develop it, acknowledges it as »their own« – and in this way preserves it.

There is no single expression to describe the purposes that this open space in the middle of the city has been put since then. But let's try: it is a paradise for kitesurfing / walking / cycling / cross-country skiing / kite-flying / barbecueing / lazing / cloud-watching / inline-skating / model-aircraft-flying.

And it is planned to stay that way. In future too visitors are intended to play a part in the reshaping of Tempelhof airfield. And these visitors are seemingly less interested in what their new park should look like than in how they can use it. People can look at natural features all over the world today, but in their city there is one thing they want above all: open spaces without flower beds, restricting architecture or additional events.

The name of the new park is thus a fitting one: Tempelhofer Freiheit (»freedom«). Fitting, not only because the endless concrete strip of runway always evokes longings to be far away, and the desire to simply fly off.

Address Tempelhofer Damm (opposite number 104), 12099 Berlin-Tempelhof (further entrances: Columbiadamm, Oderstrasse) | Transport S 41, S 42, S 46, S 47 to Tempelhof; U 6 to Tempelhof or Paradestrasse; bus 140, 184 to Tempelhofer Damm station and subway | Tip Laughing in the park: every Sunday at 12 noon the society named »Hauptstadt lacht« (»laughing capital«) meets beneath the trees near the beer garden (from October to April every fourth Sunday in the month).

106__The Terrace on the Weissensee

A trip to the lake

Lettering can be aggressive and pushy when it is intended to sell products. On the other hand, lettering can also quietly encourage you to go out and do something. For example the flowing letters in the style of handwriting on the flat roof above the terrace on the Weissensee lake. The lettering looks as simple and distinctive as the 1960s building that it adorns. Between the trees on the shore, its white letters glow invitingly out over the lake: Milchhäuschen (»dairy«).

This name was not simply invented by somebody. There is a history behind it: back in the days of the imposing Schloss Weissensee, an old manor house which in the 19th century was turned into an amusement park with slides, carousels, dance halls, taverns, and of course the famous terrace on the lake, a summer house stood in the park on the opposite side of the lake. During the First World War the manor house was burned down almost entirely, but the summer house survived the blaze. The city authorities then used the building as a place to store milk for children from needy families. Dairies in which milk produced by cows in the surrounding area could be collected and cooled were not uncommon at that time. According to some texts, the dairy in Weissensee was also used as a store for mother's milk taken from wet nurses and supplied to babies in the nearby hospital.

This is how the summer house got its name. Today the dairy and its terrace are as much a part of Weissensee as the water in the fountains in the middle of the lake. In the 1960s the old summer house had to be demolished, and the new dairy was built. The terrace remained. Bertolt Brecht and Helene Weigel lived here on the shore of the Weissensee in a house with the address Berliner Allee 185.

Today there is lots happening on the lake: boat hire, Weissensee bathing beach and a petting zoo.

Address Milchhäuschen, Parkstrasse 33 A, 13086 Berlin-Weissensee | **Transport** Tram M 4, M 13, 12 to Albertinenstrasse; bus 156 to Rennbahnstrasse / Parkstrasse; bus 158 to Parkstrasse / Amalienstrasse; bus 255 to Albertinenstrasse | **Opening times** Daily 10am – 11pm | **Tip** The sun dial: when you walk around the Weissensee lake, you will see a magnificent sundial with a diameter of ten metres amongst a display of summer flowers.

107__The Test Weight
Tangible megalomania

For many years this circular colossus was an unsolved riddle. There were many attempts to explain the huge lump of concrete among small gardens: a bunker, a water tower, a defensive position. But none of these proposals was convincing, because the true explanation for the monstrosity consisting of 12,650 tons of concrete was simply unimaginable. Until the plans were discovered.

The outsized mass was intended to test the ground for a completely unprecedented project. According to plans made by Albert Speer, the National Socialist general inspector of building works, a 117-metre-high triumphal arch was to be built on this spot for Hitler's new capital city, Germania.

Its north-south axis would have led beneath the arch to the so-called Hall of the People, the world's largest building holding 180,000 people. When Albert Speer showed his father a model of Germania, Speer senior is said to have told his son: »You have completely taken leave of your senses.«

Nevertheless, this madness had such realistic traits that Speer left nothing to chance. He had the block of concrete cast between April and October 1941 — in order to subject the ground at this place, which consisted partly of clay and was therefore difficult to calculate, to the weight of the planned building

It was and is impossible to blow up this structure or to remove it in any other way, so it remains as a reminder of the monstrous plans for the site.

Over the years it has gathered nicknames such as »mushroom«, »Nazi dumpling« or »experimental victory block«. The viewing tower on site gives an idea of the full extent of the madness: the ground was to be raised to this height, 14 metres, for the main axis passing through Berlin. The test weight would have been covered up — but all the houses between Tempelhofer Feld and Hauptstrasse would also have made way for the megalomania.

Address General Pape-Strasse 60, 12101 Berlin-Tempelhof | Transport S 1 to Julius-Leber-Brücke (10 minutes' walk); bus 104 to Kolonnenbrücke | Opening times April–Oct Wed 10am–6pm, Thu 10am–2pm, Sun 1–4pm; tours Sun 12 noon (no booking required) | Tip Papestrasse history trail: a trail through the past starts at Kolonnenbrücke and leads to the Südbahnhof in 14 stages.

108 The Teufelsberg
Winter sports on the rubble

In spring Berliners go out into the countryside, and in summer too city dwellers flock to the numerous lakes of Brandenburg, but in winter one place above all exerts a magnetic attraction on recreation-seekers: the Teufelsberg (Devil's Hill). The highest point on the sandy soils of the Brandenburg plain, proudly reaching 114.7 metres above sea level, it was built after the Second World War from 25 million cubic metres of rubble.

The idea was to create a winter sports area for the people of West Berlin: a ski jump was built, a sledge run opened, and there was even a plan to build a T-bar lift on the so-called ski slope and a building on the summit. Nothing came of the plan for a fashionable winter sports centre, however, as the Allies built a listening post at the top of the mound of rubble. Nevertheless, Berliners still come here for sledging, with and without sledges. All kinds of slideable items can be seen on the slope. Boards with rubber tyres, skateboards without their wheels, or that tried-and-tested old favourite, the plastic bag. The slopes get crowded. »Watch out!« is the cry that can be heard on all sides of the hill.

On the side where the winter sun sets in the afternoon, the domes of the radar station rise over Berlin's Grunewald forest, looking like golf balls. The white cladding of these spherical structures hangs down ragged in places. After the departure of the Allies, there was a plan to convert the spheres into luxury loft apartments. Then the film director David Lynch wanted to collaborate with an Indian guru to open a peace university with meditation courses on the top of the hill.

However, the structures are still abandoned. A leaning sign advertising the loft apartments announces that they will be completed in 2002. Everything is fenced off. All the same, it does not seem to be difficult to gain access – as demonstrated by all the tracks in the snow.

Address Teufelsseechaussee, from the car park on the right, 14055 Berlin-Charlottenburg |
Transport S 9, S 75 to Heerstrasse; bus M 49, X 34, X 49, 218 to Heerstrasse station (15 min-
utes' walk) | Tip Tours of the Western Allies' abandoned listening post are held every Sun-
day. In summer concerts are held beneath the dome of the large radar tower. For information
see www.berlinsightout.de

109_ The Tram Simulator

Watch out for people turning left

The simulator looks like a space capsule on an alien planet, as if it were waiting to be taken back to its mother ship. Inside the capsule is the driver's cockpit of a Berlin tram. As soon as you sit on the sprung seat, through both windows you see traffic starting to rush past.

Cars indicate and overtake, and the symbol on the traffic lights for trams switches from a vertical to a horizontal line. Glance in the mirror, carefully push the lever to »drive« – and you start to move with a noticeable rattle.

You pass Hackescher Markt at a leisurely pace, set the points to »right turn« at the next bend, and turn into Oranienburgerstrasse. Then all at once a car drives onto the tramlines from the right – and it's too late! There is a loud crash, you stamp on the brakes – and a black patch spreads across the monitor with dramatic slowness. You look around helplessly. Then a voice comes out of a loudspeaker in the cabin: What happened there? Didn't you see the car?

Now he makes his first appearance: the driving instructor, who is sitting at screens behind a window higher up. He not only monitors the tram's journey, but also controls what goes on in the traffic. This simulator operated by Berlin's transport authority BVG is normally used for training tram drivers. The examination candidates who take a seat in the cabin get to know the city's network of tracks and learn how to cope with unexpected situations.

If you were taking a test, you could be sure that the car that just turned left and caused an accident would reappear a few streets further ahead.

The streets of Berlin have been replicated one-to-one in the simulator: rows of houses, shops, advertising hoardings and of course the tram stops.

The best thing of all is that you can simply delete a traffic hold-up and change quickly to a different location.

Address Siegfriedstrasse 30, 10365 Berlin-Lichtenberg | Transport Tram 18, 21, 37, bus 240, 256 to Betriebshof Lichtenberg | Opening times Every 2nd and 4th Thursday in the month, tel. 030/25630333 for bookings | Tip Tierpark Berlin: a few tram stops further is Tierpark Berlin, Europe's biggest landscape zoo around Schloss Friedrichsfelde.

110__ The Uferhallen

Space for art and industrial atmosphere

One day they had all left. The last tram and the last double-decker bus drove out of the shed, the traffic lights at the gates stopped changing colour, and the buzzing neon lamps beneath the ceiling illuminated nothing more than abandoned rails and yellow markings on the ground.

The Uferhallen, the main workshops of the Berlin transport authority, closed down. It was not long before new plans had been made for what had originally been built in the 1920s for horse-drawn trams. Supermarkets and discounters were to provide the district of Wedding with a central shopping area and lots of parking spaces on this enormous site.

Fortunately, another solution was found. In 2007 a company called the Uferhallen Aktiengesellschaft was founded. It bought the site with its brick buildings on either side of Uferstrasse. Artists moved into the workshop halls – and today the space is used for music, rehearsals and creative work. In the 2500-square-metre engine hall, partitions are being moved for an exhibition, from a neighbouring hall piano music can be heard, and dancers are practising in the studios at the front.

Here on the banks of the Panke the old and the new are slowly joining together. A feeling remains of how things were in the early days. In the engine hall a huge pipe hangs from the ceiling, as if it were still in use. The clocks at the end of the hall stopped one after another, each one at a different time. One gate further along, meanwhile, there is no more room at the counter of the Waschbar, so great are the crowds around the bar in this tiled room.

The Uferhallen Aktiengesellschaft had an idea for the long-term financing of the halls. It got the artists to design shares (Aktien). All purchasers of one of these works of art become joint owners of the site – to be precise, they each own 11.5 square metres of the Uferhallen.

Address Uferstrasse 8–11, 13357 Berlin-Wedding | Transport U 8, U 9 to Osloer Strasse;
bus 125, 128, 150, 255 to Osloer Strasse subway station | Opening times For the latest
events and exhibitions, see www.uferhallen.de or tel. 030/46906871 | Tip The porter's lodge:
next to the sign »Schritt fahren« (walking speed), Café Pförtner serves good salads and other
dishes.

111_Wikingerufer

Holiday greetings, sent from home

In recent years a rather strange holiday atmosphere has been lent to the banks of the river Spree in summer. Sand is dumped, deck chairs are lined up in rows, sponsored sunshades and palm trees in tubs are arranged around them.

With few exceptions the beach bars in Berlin have lost their originality, and it has to be asked whether people really need this beach club or island atmosphere in order to enjoy a summer evening by the water.

One place makes a plea not to lose sight of the beauty that lies on your doorstep. Wikingerufer is situated on a bend in the river. The Spree snakes outwards from the city centre here. The brick-built Gebauer-Höfe on the opposite bank, bathed in the play of evening light from the sky, radiate a glowing atmosphere of romantic industrial monuments – and a smell of fresh coffee wafts over from the roasting plant within their old walls.

The three benches that stand on the bank are placed far enough apart to give you the impression of being all alone on this curve of the Spree. Local residents come with wine, glasses and picnic blankets, and sit down in front of their houses.

But Wikingerufer also has a few hidden, exclusive places to sit. Behind the gates in the railings, steps lead down to the water. The flat space halfway down the stairs is an excellent spot for a picnic. Excursion boats chug around the old industrial buildings, and the wind carries snatches of commentary across the water from their loudspeakers, telling of this history of the textile and engineering works that used to be housed there.

Then it gets quieter, the swallows stop flying their low circles over the water, and the contours of the factory chimneys become indistinct. A full moon rises over the roofs. It does this every evening here: after dark, the illuminated dome on the roof of the Technical University is almost indistinguishable from the real moon.

Address Wikingerufer, 10555 Berlin-Tiergarten | **Transport** U 9 to Hansaplatz (10 minutes' walk); bus 106 to Zinsendorfstrasse; bus 101, 245 to Franklinstrasse | **Tip** Walk by the river: you can stroll from Wikingerufer to the government quarter on the banks of the Spree – and further.

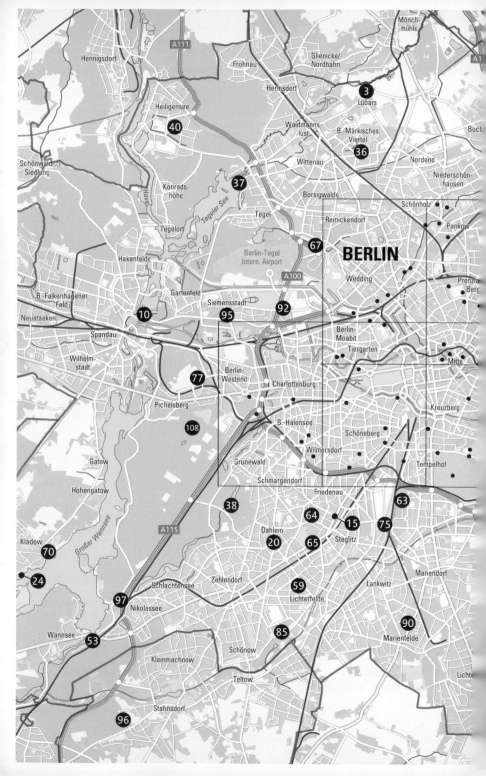

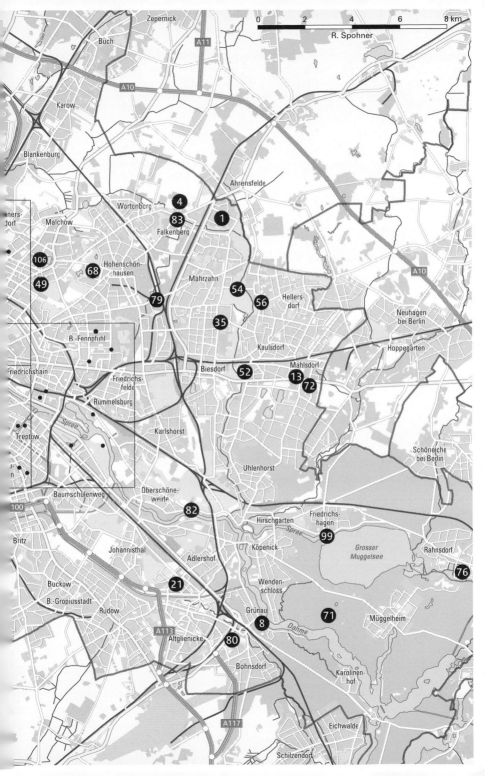

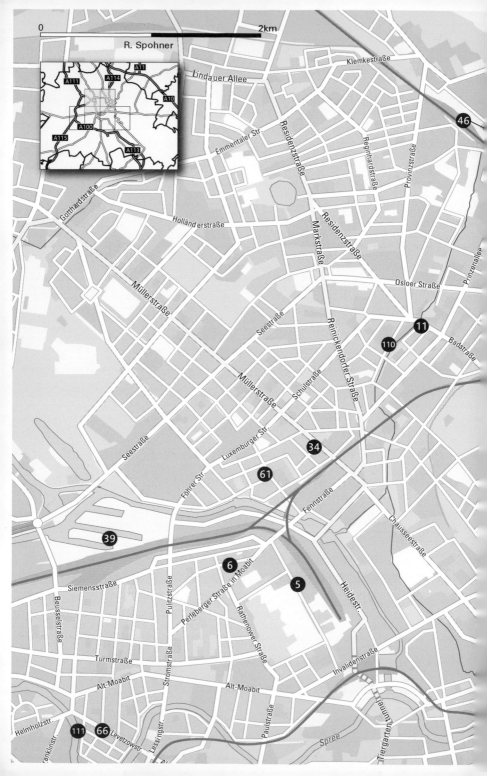

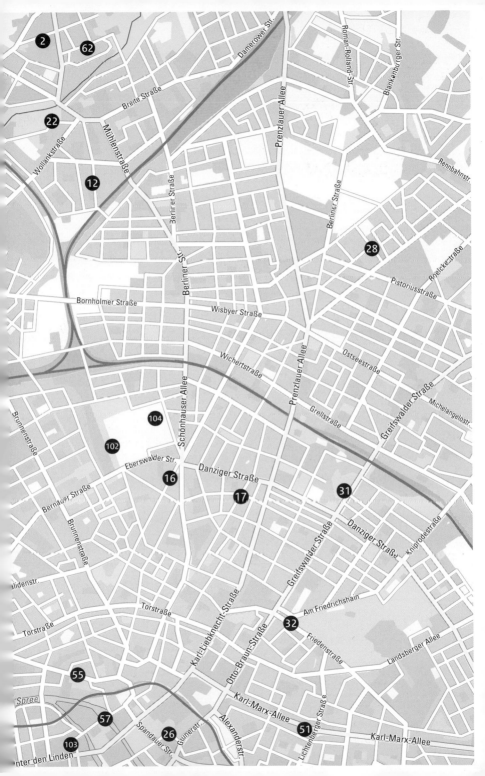

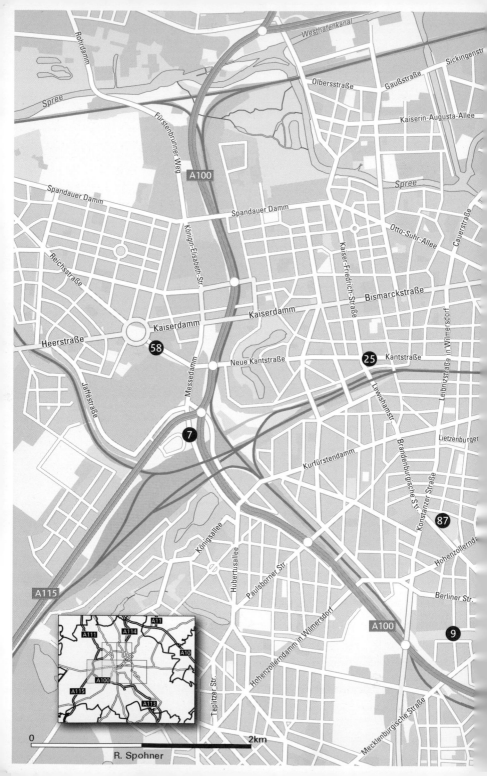

Westhafenkanal

Rohrdamm

Sickingenstr.

Olbersstraße

Gaußstraße

Kaiserin-Augusta-Allee

Spree

Fürstenbrunner Weg

A100

Spandauer Damm

Spandauer Damm

Otto-Suhr-Allee

Spree

Königin-Elisabeth-Str.

Cauerstraße

Kaiser-Friedrich-Straße

Bismarckstraße

Reichsstraße

Kaiserdamm

Kaiserdamm

58

Heerstraße

Neue Kantstraße

25

Kantstraße

Leibnizstraße in Wilmersdorf

Messedamm

Jafféstraße

7

Lewishamstr.

Lietzenburger

Kurfürstendamm

Brandenburgische Str.

Konstanzer Straße

87

A115

Königsallee

Hubertusallee

Paulsborner Str.

Hohenzollerndamm

Berliner Str.

A100

Hohenzollerndamm in Wilmersdorf

9

Teplitzer Str.

Mecklenburgische Straße

A11

A111

A114

A10

A100

A115

A113

0

2km

R. Spohner

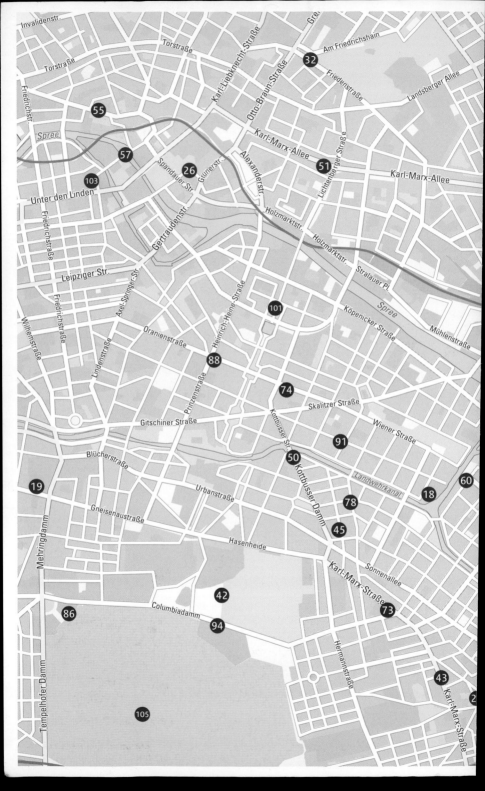